P9-CJV-594

Diagnosis and Treatment of Substance-Related Disorders

The DECLARE Model

Diagnosis and Treatment of Substance-Related Disorders

The DECLARE Model

Purcell Taylor

University of Cincinnati

Boston ■ New York ■ San Francisco
Mexico City ■ Montreal ■ Toronto ■ London ■ Madrid ■ Munich
Paris ■ Hong Kong ■ Singapore ■ Tokyo ■ Cape Town ■ Sydney

Executive Editor: *Virginia Lanigan*
Editorial Assistant: *Scott Blaszak*
Marketing Manager: *Tara Whorf*
Editorial–Production Service: *Matrix Productions Inc.*
Composition and Prepress Buyer: *Linda Cox*
Manufacturing Buyer: *Andrew Turso*
Cover Administrator: *Kristina Mose-Libon*
Illustrations: *Omegatype Typography, Inc.*
Electronic Composition: *Omegatype Typography, Inc.*

For related titles and support materials, visit our online catalog at www.ablongman.com.

Between the time Website information is gathered and then published, it is not unusual for some sites to have closed. Also, the transcription of URLs can result in unintended typographical errors. The publisher would appreciate notification where these errors occur so that they may be corrected in subsequent editions.

Library of Congress Cataloging-in-Publication Data

Taylor, Purcell.
  Diagnosis and treatment of substance-related disorders : The DECLARE
Model / Purcell Taylor.
     p. cm.
  Includes bibliographical references and index.
  ISBN 0-205-40440-5
     1. Substance abuse—Handbooks, manuals, etc. 2. Substance abuse—Patients—
Counseling of—Handbooks, manuals, etc. 3. Substance abuse—Patients—
Rehabilitation—Handbooks, manuals, etc. I. Title.

RC564.15.T39 2004
616.86'06—dc22

                                                            2004040067

Printed in the United States of America

10   9   8   7   6   5   4   3   2   1   09   08   07   06   05   04

Dedication

This book is dedicated to alcoholics and addicts everywhere, but especially to those persons who have allowed me to enter into their world of addiction. I am hopeful that DECLARE Therapy will represent for them, and for those who treat them, a hopeful path to ongoing quality sobriety and a return to living life as healthfully and as happily as possible.

In Memory of
Dr. David L. Johnson
1952–2002

CONTENTS

PREFACE

In spite of efforts to confront the issue on every front—societal, medical, personal—drug abuse in America only continues to escalate. The scourge of chemical dependency afflicts our society indiscriminately. No socioeconomic or ethnic group is immune. Treatment methods abound, in fact multiply, but few to date have been shown to address adequately the multiple causes and consequences of substance abuse. Responding to this urgent need, I brought my own and others' extensive experience and expertise to bear in the search for a comprehensive and flexible treatment methodology that would allow for intervention on many levels, offer specific procedures for compiling information, and provide clinicians with a schema that is easy to remember and simple to administer.

DECLARE Therapy is the result of this search and fulfills all of these criteria. I invite you to examine this timely and effective therapeutic approach.

Acknowledgments

This text could not have been written without the generous support and encouragement of many of my family, friends, colleagues, and teachers. I wish to thank Dr. Vera C. Edwards, Dr. Eula Bingham, the late Dr. Barry Lehrer, Dr. Venus Bluestein, Mr. William Barkley, Dr. Marty Sapp, Dean Marilyn Smith, Professor George Prather, Mr. Bob Ross, and Ms. Leah Menninger for their contributions.

I especially acknowledge the late Dr. David L. Johnson for the many hours we spent listening to each others' ideas on chemical dependency and for giving me the encouragement to stay the course. His contributions to the text are greatly appreciated.

My gratitude is also extended to Dr. Arnold Lazarus, A.B.P.P., for his most valuable manuscript critique, and to Rose Huber for editorial expertise.

I am also grateful to the reviewers of this book: George M. Andrews, Baltimore City Community College; Thomas Czerlinsky, Thomas University; Samuel S. Faulkner, Morehead State University; Richard W. Greenlee, Ohio University; C. Brett Hendricks, Texas Tech University; Carolyn Stone, University of North Florida; and Charles A. Weiner, Henderson State University.

Finally, I thank my wife, Leslye, who has stood with me through the many years it has taken to develop this book. She has been and continues to be a source of support and encouragement.

Purcell Taylor, Jr., Ed.D., D.A.B.P.S.
April 2003

ABOUT THE AUTHOR

Dr. Purcell Taylor is currently the Director of the Sex Offender Program for the Center for Children and Families and was formerly the Clinical Service Director of Saint Francis Academy's Sex Offender and Victims Programs in Cincinnati, Ohio. Over the course of his thirty years of clinical experience, he has worked as Clinical Director of a Halfway House within the Ohio Department of Rehabilitation and Corrections; Sex Offender Violence and Treatment Professional; Forensic Assessment and Treatment Consultant for the Institute for Psychiatry and Law at the University of Cincinnati Medical School; Dual Disorders Therapist and Chemical Dependency Therapist; Assistant Superintendent of the Longview State Hospital for the State of Ohio's Department of Mental Health; and Superintendent of the Broadview Development Center with the Ohio Department of Mental Retardation and Development Disabilities. He holds a doctoral degree in School Psychology from the University of Cincinnati.

Dr. Taylor currently is an Associate Professor of Psychology and Psychiatry at the University of Cincinnati Psychology Department, College of Arts and Sciences, and teaches both graduate and undergraduate students. He has also taught at several other universities. Dr. Taylor has coauthored several publications on sex offenders and has authored several books on chemical dependency. He also has publications and research reports in related areas.

Dr. Taylor is a member of the Association for the Treatment of Sexual Abusers, the American Psychological Association, the Ohio Psychological Association, and the American College of Forensic Examiners and is a Diplomate of the American Board of Psychological Specialties with a Forensic Specialty in Clinical Psychology. He is a Licensed Professional Clinical Counselor and a Certified Chemical Dependency Counselor III-E with Clinical Endorsement. Dr. Taylor's research interests include stress and its psychophysiological effects, phenomenology and treatment of chemical dependency, phenomenology and treatment of sex offenders, and the development of chemical dependency assessment instruments.

Dr. Taylor has developed several sex offender and chemical dependency treatment programs at both state and local levels. He has served on several national editorial boards and has been called as an expert witness in forensic cases. Dr. Taylor has also appeared on the John Walsh show as an expert guest on the treatment of adult and adolescent sexual offenders. He has also consulted with the Montel Williams Talk Show staff regarding sexual offending behaviors. Dr. Taylor has received several awards for his professional and community activities and has appeared on local television and has been interviewed in the print media as an expert on offender issues and profiling.

INTRODUCTION

DECLARE Therapy's origin and subsequent development can be traced back to 1980 when I initially became interested in the area of substance abuse while teaching a psychology course at the University of Cincinnati. It was during this period that I recognized there were few, if any, comprehensive approaches to the assessment, diagnosis, and treatment of substance-related disorders.

Although several psychosocial treatments for drug-dependent individuals currently exist (and existed in the early 1980s and 1990s), many were initially developed for individuals with problems other than drug dependence. The drug abuse treatment community has indeed adapted many of these therapies to meet the needs of drug-dependent clients, but more needs to be accomplished in the development of new— and the modification of established—therapies for drug dependence and/or substance abuse (National Institute on Drug Abuse, 1992).

After several years of using various existing approaches with my own clients without any measurable success, I began probing for a method that would satisfy the demands of both the client and the clinician. Such a method would, ideally:

- Meet the needs of individuals with substance-related disorders
- Provide the clinician with a therapeutic approach that would allow for the assessment, diagnosis, and treatment of substance-related disorders
- Permit the clinician to use this method with his or her own flexible approach, within a biopsychosocial framework

While formulating these goals, I became increasingly aware of the need for a comprehensive approach to chemical dependency, and I recognized that the disease of chemical dependency involves an interaction of three constituent systems: the biological, the emotional/motivational, and the social. In analyzing their interaction, I then determined that the criteria for this "ideal" assessment/diagnostic/treatment method must include the following:

- Admission by the client, at some level of self-conscious awareness, that he or she is chemically dependent or has a problem with alcohol or drugs—an essential step before effective intervention can be initiated (Miller, 1991)
- A schema that is easy to remember
- A schema that is easy to administer
- Clear and effective treatment strategies

From this rudimentary outline emerged DECLARE Therapy, a mode of treatment based on seven biopsychosocial modalities, or points of entry, for viewing the problems of a client:

Denial

Esteem

Confusion

Loss of Significant Resources

Acceptance

Resolution

Entry

That is to say, the drug abuser typically:

- engages in a **D**enial of the use of alcohol/drugs
- has diminished self-**E**steem
- is **C**onfused
- has **L**ost physical, psychological, and social resources
- **A**ccepts reality of dependence on alcohol/drugs
- **R**esolves to seek therapeutic assistance
- later re-**E**nters traditional society as a chemically free individual ready to begin the lifelong process of recovery (See Figure I.1.)

DECLARE Therapy is unique in that it fits the treatment to the client rather than the client to the treatment, employing a therapeutic approach that emphasizes two basic orientations, one negative and one positive. Negative behavioral orientation (NBO) refers to behavior characterized by thoughts and feelings dwelling on failures, frustrations, and fears that culminates in a self-fulfilling prophecy of uncontrolled self-abuse through drugs despite the adverse consequences. Positive behavioral orientation (PBO) refers to the development of mediated self-control on the part of the client, who becomes overtly aware of the extent of his or her drug abuse. As we will see in Chapter 1, eliminating NBO is in fact the main target of DECLARE Therapy. Accordingly, the present text seeks to provide clinicians with a conceptual framework for persuading the substance abuser to give up his or her self-defeating behavioral orientation while redirecting the individual toward a desirable, self-fulfilling behavioral orientation.*

In effect, treatment based on the seven DECLARE modalities and NBO and PBO modalities allows for thorough quantitative and qualitative assessment of a substance abuser's biopsychosocial functioning. In addition, it provides an effective approach for the remediation of problems associated with substance-related disorders

---

*It is necessary to point out a possible confusion between the multifaceted approach of DECLARE Therapy and that of Arnold Lazarus's Multimodal therapy. Despite the parallels that can be drawn between the two methods, they are clearly distinct, with each focusing on different aspects of the human personality and its functioning.

FIGURE I.1   Psychosocial Modalities in the Treatment of Substance Abuse

Modality I—Denial

The substance abuser refuses to believe or allow awareness of the threatening or unpleasant aspects of drug abuse.

Modality II—Esteem

Issues arise concerning feelings of personal self-worth. Self-worth is defined as a basic psychological feeling that all human beings possess in varying degrees. Among those who abuse drugs, this feeling is compromised or is not present at all.

Modality III—Confusion

The drug abuser, in a chaotic and disorganized lifestyle now controlled by demands of the drugs, begins to recognize the effects of having little or no regularity or predictability concerning normal life experiences.

Modality IV—Loss of Significant Resources

Overt awareness begins to occur as the result of the loss of the drug abuser's most important possessions—e.g., health, family, friends, job, finances, legal status, etc.

Modality V—Acceptance

The drug abuser finally accepts his or her dependency on drugs by saying, "I want to stop hurting. I need help." The acceptance of a drug problem signals the beginning of the search for treatment and eventual recovery from the ravages of the effects of drugs.

Modality VI—Resolution

The individual seeks a course of action—i.e., treatment to deal with his or her drug dependency. The form resolution takes varies from person to person.

Modality VII—Entry

The client has achieved disengagement from the world of drug abuse and is now entering/reentering conventional society, in which abuse has no place. The entry/reentry process follows the Biphasic Analysis Reintegration Sequence (BARS):

    Phase I—Demonstrated disengagement from the world of drug abuse.

    Phase II—Maintenance of therapeutic gains through appropriate aftercare, which the client is unwilling to jeopardize by again becoming involved in drug-abusing behavior.

that enables clients, working closely with the clinician, to develop appropriate coping skills, styles, strategies, and interaction patterns; to reestablish proprietorship of their own thoughts and behavior; and, ultimately, to live as productively and healthfully as possible once free of the mask of abuse.

The following chapters describe in depth the various dimensions of the DECLARE therapeutic model. Incorporating elucidative diagrams, Chapter 1 describes the bio-psychosocial paradigm used to conceptualize substance abuse; Chapter 2 investigates the diverse methods and procedures used to assess the client and develop a modality profile; Chapters 3 and 4 delineate the processes of assessment, diagnosis, and treatment; and finally, Chapter 5 reveals the difficult challenges faced by individuals embarking on the lifelong process of recovery. Throughout the book, case studies illustrate the conceptual and procedural aspects of therapy and serve to highlight both its personal magnitude and exciting potentiality.

Diagnosis and Treatment of Substance-Related Disorders

The DECLARE Model

1 Overview

What's wrong with this picture?

The United States spends an estimated 50 billion dollars each year for oil. Double that figure to 100 billion dollars and you have this country's annual revenue from its illicit drug trade. Experts calculate the global trade in illegal drugs may run as high as 500 billion dollars annually. Sadly, the United States is said to have the biggest market, and even more tragically, the illicit drug trade is reported to be the fastest growing enterprise in the world today!

Unquestionably, illegal drug trafficking is the most profitable of all industries currently in operation. A handful of Latin American countries grow coca that yields cocaine. In Asia, the harvesting of opium poppy for conversion into heroin is reaching record amounts. And marijuana flourishes everywhere.

Is it any wonder that the pervasiveness of the illegal drug trade, along with the criminality associated with it, appears to have overwhelmed both our government and our citizenry? Is it any wonder that drug abuse has become one of our country's most devastating embarrassments?

The multifold effects of drug abuse in the United States constitute a major public health enigma that exerts a heavy toll on our society in terms of economic costs and human suffering (Taylor, 1988a; Taylor, 1982; Califano, 1979; Mayer, 1983; Quayle, 1983; Matsunaga, 1983; Lubin et al., 1986; French et al., 1996; Goodwin & Gabriell, 1997; U.S. Department of Health and Human Services, 1991; NIDA, 2003). Literally millions of people suffer from the chemical effects of one or more types of substances—a situation that remains intractable in the face of efforts to treat the biopsychosocial dimensions of substance abuse. Few treatment methods currently in use have achieved significant success with substance-related disorders, and the number of reported treatment failures only continues to increase (Craig, 1987; Miller & Hester, 1986). Treatment approaches have also been multiplying, but cure rates are still not encouraging. The few follow-up studies that have been conducted indicate that only about 40 percent of drug abusers remain permanently abstinent after treatment (Bootzin et al., 1993).

It has been estimated that approximately 85 percent of all alcohol and drug abusers, both young and old, are polysubstance users and/or abusers but, interestingly

1

enough, not necessarily addicts. Clearly, our society has paid the price for this 1980s age of sedativism and polysubstance abuse. That price is a prevalent disease called chemical dependency.

High-Tech, Low-Contact Reality

Without doubt, the decade of the 1980s was the decade of polydrug abuse. Regrettably, the trend toward polydrug abuse that escalated in the 1980s continued to manifest itself in the 1990s—a decade that will, no doubt, go down in the annals of behavioral health history as the age of stress and depression. Just take a look at what's happening within our society as we enter the twenty-first century.

Our emphasis on high-tech living has resulted in interpersonal relationships devoid of meaningful contact. We find ourselves in a depersonalized world where societal decadence and a lack of acceptable goals and values appear to be the norm within some circles. Is it any wonder, then, that so many of us need a boost to our self-esteem? Or search for aids to mental clarity and functioning? Understandably, many frustrated and confused individuals turn to alcohol and drugs as positive, mood-altering substances. If present trends continue, this will undoubtedly be the case for some time to come.

If we accept this scenario as accurate, we are left with a logical conclusion: *It becomes essential for society to answer the challenge of illicit substance abuse with positive, proactive responses that persuade individuals not to abuse alcohol and drugs in the first place.*

The DECLARE Model

Because it represents at once a nonlinear, multifaceted, cognitive-behavioral, proactive approach, DECLARE Therapy can be a viable and effective means to answering the challenge of chemical dependency (Figure 1.1). Essentially, it presents a results-oriented approach to the assessment, diagnosis, and treatment of substance-related disorders that is based on a three-part commitment. As shown in Figure 1.2, this model contains:

1. A paradigm for conceptualizing substance-related disorders
2. A treatment procedure
3. A method for the pursuit of scientific inquiry into the etiology, diagnosis, treatment, disengagement, reintegration, and aftercare of persons with substance-related disorders

It is important to keep these three aspects of the model distinct, as comments or criticisms appropriate to one may not be relevant to the other(s). However, the clinician must also keep in mind the links between them.

Definition	Course	Treatment
Chemical dependency is a primary, often chronically learned set of negative behaviors that are characterized by continuous or episodic impaired control over drug use. There is compulsion to use the drug despite the negative consequences. Distortions in the cognitive, emotional, and behavioral spheres occur, resulting, most notably, in denial, diminished self-esteem, confusion, and loss of significant resources.	Chemical dependency is a complex set of interactions between biological, psychological, and social factors over time. Those who demonstrate a vulnerability to develop chemical dependency and abuse may potentially become chemically dependent.	Multifaceted in approach, treatment is determined individually according to the causal and maintaining factors revealed in the modality profile.

FIGURE 1.1   DECLARE Model of Chemical Dependency

Contained within the three-part model of DECLARE Therapy is a bio-psychosocial conceptualization, or paradigm, of substance-related disorders that is based on three perspectives, which, in turn, can be subdivided into various components. This paradigm can be outlined as follows:

A. Micropsychological Perspective
    1. Biopsychological Dimension
        a. Neuronal effects
        b. Structural effects
    2. Intrapersonal dimension (information processing)
B. Macropsychosocial Perspective
    1. Dynamic Tension
    2. Declatype and Declatypical Syndromes
    3. Entopsychic Processes
    4. Negative Behavioral Orientation (NBO)
    5. Positive Behavioral Orientation (PBO)
C. Metapsychological Perspective
    1. Transcendental Experience
    2. Churchill Syndrome

Note the references to "Declatypes," "Declatypical syndromes," and "entopsychic processes." The following sections will elucidate these terms, which were coined in the development of the DECLARE therapeutic model, and explain the ramifications of the biopsychosocial paradigm.

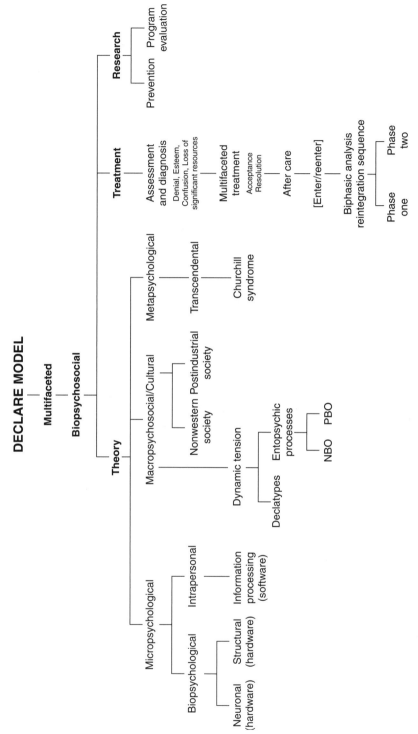

FIGURE 1.2 DECLARE Therapy: Theory, Treatment, and Research

Micropsychological Perspective

Neuronal Effects.   The micropsychological perspective emphasizes the biological effects of drugs on the brain's information processing. To picture what takes place, envision the brain in terms of a computer information system. The neuronal component (the "hardware") affects the turnover of all neurotransmitters and neuropeptides (the "software"), which are linked through a network of feedback control mechanisms that normally maintains a state of equilibrium. Drugs can disrupt this equilibrium on both levels.

Keep in mind that the author conceptualizes addiction as an experience that shares properties with that of chronic pain (Bellissimo & Turk, 1984; Turk et al., 1983). Consequently, addiction may be viewed from a "gate control model" perspective. In other words, an individual experiences addiction whenever a set of neural "gates" opens that lead specifically to the substance of abuse.

As these neural gates open, the neural cells specific to the drug abused exceed their predetermined limits (in terms of their activity) and a system is set into motion— a system that produces addiction. The initiation of this systemic activity causes a motor and autonomic dysfunction that provides further sensory input, which, in turn, assists in establishing the vicious cycle of addiction.

At any given point during the development of addiction, the abuser moves into what we may appropriately term the Valley of Tears Syndrome (VTS), which refers to a biopsychological dimension of despair, loss of personal dignity, fear, and loneliness. Every chemically dependent person must pass through this dimension on the journey to addiction, and no victim can return from this journey without intervention (Taylor, 1988b; Cloninger, 1988; Pickins & Svikis, 1988; Alcoholics Anonymous, 1976).

During this precarious pilgrimage to self-destruction, euphoria typically gives way to dysphoria, which leads to even more frequent ingestion of the substance being abused in a (generally futile) attempt to restore the diminishing euphoria. As the addiction progresses, the dysphoric stage becomes the dominant stage, and the euphoric stage is seldom achieved, if at all (Schuckit, 1989).

Structural Effects.   Structurally, interference in brain functioning is seen at the organizational level, where information processing is altered by the

- *Reticular activating system:* alert system of the brain
- *Hypothalamus:* part of the brain controlling emotions, thirst, hunger, sex
- *Hippocampus:* part of the brain involved in memory
- *Medial forebrain bundle:* "feel-good system" of the brain; part of limbic system
- *Periventricular system:* punishment center of the brain
- *Basal ganglia:* part of the brain involved in gross motor movement and posture; located in frontal lobe
- *Cerebral cortex:* upper level of the brain involved in thinking, learning, remembering

Whenever the specialized functions of these structures are altered by drugs, they produce neuropsychological anomalies resulting in behavioral alterations that can include any or all of the following:

- Impairment of normal patterns of sleep
- Alteration of arousal and awareness
- Distortion of sensory perception
- Impairment of psychomotor performance
- Motor incoordination and/or tremor
- Impairment of memory and/or learning
- Increased anxiety
- Inappropriate behavior(s)
- Reduction of motivation
- Mood changes

These symptoms are directly related to the respective biochemical changes induced by the drug at the neuronal and structural levels of the brain (Nahas & Frick II, 1981).

When substance abuse advances to this stage, the abuser is no longer making a cognitive choice to ingest the alcohol or drugs because of a bad marriage or peer pressure or whatever conditions and motivations first tempted him or her to turn to the chemical(s) in question. The user-turned-abuser now *needs* the substance and, typically, will engage in antisocial and/or criminal behavior to obtain it (Alterman et al., 1998; Koster & Rounsaville, 1986, Meyer & Mirin, 1979; Gilbert & Lombardi, 1967; Leshner 1999).

Interestingly (and this should be kept in mind as you progress through this book), once the individual reaches this stage of abuse, the addiction experienced is not for the drug per se, but rather for the *feelings* the chemical produces.

At this stage, anatomical, biochemical, and bioelectrical effects may be observed that differ from those manifested at earlier, cognitively controlled stages of the drug-taking behavior. Essentially, for those who suffer from the disease of chemical dependency, the message to take the drug results in compulsive and noncontrolled behavior (Taylor, 1988b).

Use, Abuse, and Vulnerability.   The tendency to use and abuse drugs is related to the following vulnerability factors:

- Vulnerability to use one of the mood-altering substances (e.g., the availability of the drug)
- Vulnerability to use a drug for other than medicinal purposes (i.e., abuse that results in the impaired physical, social, mental, and emotional well-being of the user)
- Vulnerability to develop the disease because of physical (e.g., anatomical, biochemical), genetic, psychological, and social factors

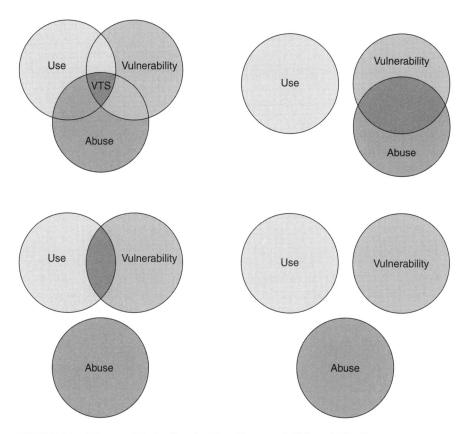

FIGURE 1.3   Diagram Illustrating the Use, Abuse, and Vulnerability Concept
(From Taylor, 1988b. Courtesy of Charles C. Thomas, Publisher, Springfield, Illinois.)

One way to visualize the relationship among use, abuse, and vulnerability is with the use of moving, at times overlapping, circles, each representing one of the three variables (Figure 1.3). The area where all three overlap may be thought of as the Valley of Tears Syndrome.

In viewing the illustration, it is helpful to think of each circle as moving away from or toward the others, depending on the relative importance of each of the three variables. The circles/variables are in constant and fluid motion, their size and significance changing over time.

Note that, symbolically, when no overlap occurs between Vulnerability and the other circles, or variables, addiction does not occur. The same is true when Use moves independently, without incidence of overlap. According to this dynamic, addiction (symbolized by VTS) only occurs when all three circles overlap. Obviously drug use plays a major contributory role in the development of the disease of chemical dependency, because, simply stated: You can't abuse unless you use!

In theory, a person might be able to withstand the effects of high use if the individual's abuse and vulnerability were quite low. As can be shown by an analogous configuration of the circles (ready to converge), however, the person now would be set for development of the disease of chemical dependency.

To understand the potential effectiveness of DECLARE Therapy, using the micropsychological perspective, it is helpful once again to envision the brain's information-processing system in terms of a computer. Whenever interference (due to substance abuse) occurs at the neuronal or structural ("hardware") levels, the equilibrium of the brain's information-processing system is altered, resulting in cognitive and/or behavioral anomalies analogous to "error messages" in a computer. In the brain, such messages become interpreted as noncontrolled, drug-taking behavior.

Macropsychosocial Perspective

According to the macropsychosocial perspective of DECLARE Therapy, disturbance of psychic forces within the personality that maintain substance-abusing behavior—forces termed *entopsychic*—gives rise to certain patterns of behavior—termed *Declatypes*—that are associated with faulty cognitions in memory, perceptions, language, problem solving, and/or abstract thinking. To ameliorate these dysfunctional patterns of thinking and behaving, it is necessary for the substance abuser to reestablish entopsychic equilibrium and to develop a new set of coping skills in traditional society.

Figure 1.4 illustrates the relationship between entopsychic forces and Declatypical behavior in a person abusing mind-altering drugs. The wavy line serves to denote the dynamic tension characterizing entopsychic imbalance.

Negative Declatypes

Negative Declatypes are negative patterns of behavior displayed by substance abusers in one or more of the following areas:

- Conscious awareness
- Sexuality
- Family
- Expression of feelings
- Social status
- Behavior
- Social skills
- Denial

More specifically, they refer to negative behaviors that are displayed by those who use mind-altering drugs *despite* adverse consequences and that can be grouped according

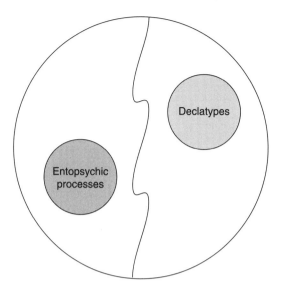

**FIGURE 1.4   Macropsychosocial Model Illustrating
the Concept of Dynamic Tension and Entopsychic
Balance**

to four basic modalities: Denial, Esteem, Confusion, and Loss of Significant Resources. These predictable negative patterns are universal—that is, abusers possess a psychosocial predisposition to behave in these specific ways.

Negative Declatypical Syndromes.   The constellations that serve to inform the various Declatypes can be *operationally* defined as *Declatypical syndromes.* Ironically, these syndromes seem to be apparent to everyone but the abuser. That is because the abuser is so strongly preoccupied with drug-abusing behavior that he or she is incapable of thinking about anything other than getting the next fix or high.

Virtually every addict's Declatype acts as an infrastructure—an infrastructure associated with relevant experiences that conclusively form a syndrome. After gaining sufficient strength from the accumulation of experiences, the syndrome finds expression.

Consider, for example, the development of a Declatypical syndrome out of the Declatype of Denial. As the person experiences more events in his or her drug-abusing world, those experiences that are relevant to the Denial Declatype become attached to it to form the Denial Declatypical Syndrome. As a result, the syndrome becomes stronger and stronger by virtue of the accumulation of new experiences.

If the Denial Declatypical Syndrome becomes dominant, then much of what the person experiences and how he or she behaves is governed by the syndrome. In other words, the abuser organizes every aspect of life in ways that prevent awareness of the threatening or unpleasant aspects of the noncontrolled, drug-abusing behavior and that secure an attitude of oblivious disregard to the concerns of others. In essence, the syndrome of *denial* seizes control of the entire life and personality of the abuser.

As mentioned earlier, denial is just one example of four central negative Declatypical syndromes that control an abuser's thoughts and actions in an extreme, often unlimited, capacity:

- Denial
- Esteem
- Confusion
- Loss of Significant Resources

These four syndromes present themselves during the assessment and diagnostic stages of therapy. To understand some of the basic dynamics of DECLARE Therapy, let's look at the four negative Declatypical syndromes in terms of actual case studies.

Case Study: Denial. W.R. is a 34-year-old African-American male who reports a seventeen-year history of drug abuse. At 17, he began to gradually abuse alcohol (which he currently drinks to excess several days per week).

He also reports that about six years ago, he used heroin and cocaine intravenously—a habit that resulted in his hospitalization for treatment of a fungus infection in the right lung. He says he currently abuses his prescription drug (Tylenol with codeine) and alcohol (consuming 80 oz. a day). Assessment further reveals he has experienced eight separate incidences of "overdoses" in the past eight years.

Currently, W.R. indicates that he spends only thirty dollars per month on drugs. Given his past behavior, the reported amount of money spent should be viewed cautiously. He also admits to having engaged in illegal activities for profit during the past thirty days.

Despite his current circumstances, W.R. does not regard himself as being an alcoholic and/or drug dependent. He says he uses drugs to "relax" or "unwind," to "feel adequate," to "feel more accepted by others," to "avoid things," to "think" and to "get to sleep." He also states that he uses drugs when he is angry, depressed, worried, tired, and/or lonely.

This client's seventeen-year history of drug abuse appears to represent an attempt to cope with entopsychic processes to alleviate his problem(s).

Case Study: Esteem. R.B. is a 41-year-old, single, disabled, unemployed African-American male who was referred for drug detoxification by a local state mental health hospital where he was receiving psychiatric treatment. R.B. states that he was seeking admission to a drug abuse treatment facility because of his thirteen-year history of polydrug abuse. During the initial interview, he explained that he is presently living with his mother in her apartment building, a situation that causes him "depression" and "frustration." He attributes these feelings, in part, to the fact that (he says) his mother treats him "like a teenager."

R.B. says that, because of what he calls his "psychological inability to say no," he allows people to use him and, consequently, finds himself doing things like running errands for others, lending money that is never repaid, and so on. He also indicates that because of what he describes as his "low self-esteem and feelings of worthlessness," he continuously wears untidy clothing—even though he does have appropriate clothing at home. This client further states that he often stops by a local tavern to have a couple of drinks during the afternoon, but never at night, due to the dress code. R.B. refuses to shave, comb his hair, and/or dress appropriately.

Because of his incurable infection of chronic hepatitis, R.B. is partially disabled and says he is limited to lifting only five pounds in weight. As a result of his disability, he is currently receiving state welfare assistance.

Case Study: Confusion.   T.R. is a 24-year-old Caucasian male who was previously involved in a drug-free counseling program for twelve months. Treatment, however, was terminated subsequent to his incarceration for probation violation. He was recently arrested for drug abuse and for resisting arrest when he was discovered "passed out" on the lot of a gasoline station. It is reported that earlier that evening he had ingested a number of Nembutal capsules and had consumed several beers at a local bar.

On T.R.'s journey home from the bar, he was arrested after he lost consciousness when walking across the lot of the gas station. Held in the city jail overnight, he was detained there for six days until his grandfather posted a $2,000 bond for his release. T.R. appeared in court and pleaded "no contest" to both charges. He now faces a possible sentence of six months for the drug abuse charge and ninety days for resisting arrest. Before sentencing T.R., the judge ordered a presentencing investigation (PSI) and referral to a local drug-counseling center. As part of the PSI, he was scheduled for a psychiatric evaluation at the court psychiatric center.

This client reports increased frequency of abusing various drugs—for example, Nembutal, Tuanol, Dilaudid, Placidyl, and Valium—after his release from prison. In 1981, he was briefly employed, but was laid off four weeks later. He is currently unemployed, and his parents were recently divorced. He believes that his parents' divorce and other "family problems" contribute to his ongoing depression.

It is obvious that T.R. has limited vocational skills—a condition that only exacerbates his difficulty in obtaining gainful employment. Although his grandparents provide him with food and shelter, he feels "trapped," engaging in virtually no social activity. He says he has few friends and is frequently depressed concerning his inability to meet people (drug free) and to establish relationships with females.

T.R. says he uses drugs in an attempt to escape his chronic feelings of depression as well as the negative feelings associated with his inability to find employment, to live apart from his relatives, and to establish an independent lifestyle free from drugs. He believes that regular counseling will be beneficial in assisting him to avoid drugs and that the counseling sessions will provide a structural setting whereby he can develop realistic plans to improve his living situation, which, he says, is presently "out of control."

Case Study: Loss of Significant Resources.   R.S. is a 19-year-old, single, Caucasian male with a ninth-grade education. He reports that, due to his excessive use of drugs and alcohol, he was not able to attend school regularly. Even when he did go, he says, he was so "stoned" that he could not concentrate on his studies. He is currently unemployed; when he is employed, it is as an unskilled laborer. He says that because of his recent unemployment problems and only for financial reasons, he is now living with a close family friend.

According to his account, this client began using marijuana when he was 10 years old and has continued to use it on a regular basis for the past nine years. He further indicates that whenever he attempts to abstain from using this illegal substance, he becomes so agitated that he loses control and sometimes becomes violent. R.S. recalls recently being hospitalized for a fractured right hand, which he suffered as a result of losing control and punching a wall. In addition, he reports having been arrested several times for drug abuse and says he has sporadically abused quaaludes and amphetamines in the past several years. R.S. says he has few friends in the "straight world" and that this is due to his use of drugs.

Acquired Declatypes

Some persons experience certain patterns of behavior because of acquired conditions such as Fetal Alcohol Syndrome (FAS), Fetal Alcohol Effect (FAE), Fetal Drug Syndrome (FDS), and Fetal Drug Effect (FDE); others, because they experienced secondary drug abuse as "cocaine/crack babies," "ice babies," or "methadone babies"; still others, because they have a constitutional vulnerability due to family history—in other words, a specific gene has been passed on.

In DECLARE Therapy, these acquired patterns of behavior, termed *acquired Declatypes,* are reservoirs of biopsychosocial symptom clusters. The development of these clusters is, of course, due to interference with the growth process during the prenatal period.

The process of human development occurs in three phases:

1. The ovum period, typically ten to fourteen days, lasting from the time of fertilization until the zygote is implanted in the uterus
2. The embryo period, lasting two to eight weeks
3. The fetus period, lasting eight to forty weeks and characterized by the growth of the organism

Even at the embryonic stage, activity is rapid. The zygote has been implanted and the egg is already beginning to differentiate itself into three distinct layers: the ectoderm, mesoderm, and endoderm. From the ectoderm will emerge the epidermis (skin), hair, parts of the teeth, skin glands, sensory cells, and the nervous system. (Elkind & Weiner, 1978; Worchel & Shebilske, 1992).

If the pregnant mother uses or abuses drugs during this developmental stage, these chemical substances may cause dramatic interference in this vital process. The babies born to drug-using mothers inherit addiction when they are conceived and experience withdrawal as soon as they are born, or shortly thereafter.

Women using phencyclidine (otherwise known as angel dust, or PCP), cocaine, or sedative-hypnotics, for example, create potential problems for their babies, who may be born with FDS, a condition that includes one or more of the following symptoms:

- Neurobehavioral abnormalities
- Congenital abnormalities
- Fetal growth retardation
- Seizures and/or convulsions
- Vomiting
- Diarrhea
- An underdeveloped respiratory system
- Blue color due to lack of oxygen
- Low birth weight
- Neonatal growth retardation

By the same token, it has become apparent that infants born to cocaine-using women are at even greater risk for various anomalies because cocaine exerts a powerful negative influence on both pregnancy outcome and on neonatal neurobehavior (Chasnoff, 1988, 2002; Weston et al., 1989; Keith et al., 1989; Gold, 1987; Van de bor et al., 1990).

The middle layer (mesoderm) forms the dermis, the muscles, the skeleton, and the circulatory and excretory systems. Should a woman use or abuse drugs at this state of development, she risks damaging the bone structure and muscle tone of the embryo.

If a woman uses or abuses drugs while the endoderm is developing, her baby runs the risk of damaging vital tissue because this layer of the embryo gives rise to the development of the lining of the entire gastrointestinal tract, as well as the eustachian tubes, trachea, bronchia, lungs, liver, pancreas, thymus, thyroid glands, and salivary glands.

For example, cigarette smoking during pregnancy would cause vasoconstriction of the woman's blood vessels, thereby creating hypoxia (lack of oxygen) and an excessive buildup of carbon monoxide, both of which have the potential to seriously impair the developing embryo. These examples of embryonic and/or fetal damage support the notion of biogenic-behavioral-teratological compromises—or acquired (passed-on genetic defects) Declatypes.

In those with acquired Declatypes, the psychosocial symptom cluster includes acquired behavior patterns in a psychosocial context—for example, induction into drug use and abuse occurs primarily when family or groups of friends push the drug(s) onto the novice.

Case Study: A Family History. N.J. is a 12-year-old Caucasian male with a three-year history of delinquent behavior. His most recent arrest was for stealing a knife and a pint of whiskey. This incident brought his case to the attention of several professional specialists in the area of alcohol and drug abuse treatment.

This youngster reports having used drugs since the age of 9 and maintains that he has experimented with several chemical substances—"pot," barbiturates, alcohol. His father states he is concerned about his son's use of drugs and believes that many of his difficulties did not emerge until he began to use these substances.

N.J. acknowledges that his drug use is a problem but reports that he has "tried to quit, but can't." He also says that once he starts taking drugs, he doesn't seem to be able to control it. As for relationships, the youngster indicates having a great deal of difficulty getting along with his mother, who is an alcoholic. Consequently, the entire family is caught up in the mother's dependency, and its members are unable to focus on the problems and concerns of N.J.

Entopsychic Processes.   In DECLARE Therapy, one of the therapist's major challenges is to assist the client in understanding the entopsychic processes that have resulted in self-destructive, abusing behavior. By the same token, the therapist must understand the client's Declatypes and how they affect certain behavior patterns and personality functioning. It is important to recognize, for instance, that the typical addict tends to conceal his or her needs and problems from others, such as family, friends, and significant others. To understand the addict and the world of the addict, the therapist must view this person from the perspective of how and why these concealments take place.

Typically, an addict attempting to cope with one or more issues of substance abuse constructs a psychic mask that seemingly protects the noncontrolled, drug-abusing behavior—a measure taken in the hopes of reducing unpleasant feelings or problems, such as anger, loneliness, isolation, sexual dysfunction(s), anxiety, resentment, depression, fear, and so forth. The intrapsychic concealment of needs and problems that are behaviorally expressed through substance abuse are referred to as *entopsychic processes,* that is, the adoption of inappropriate coping skills, styles, strategies, and interaction patterns to cope with needs and problems.

In the context of the client's world, the therapist must uncover and *reveal to the client* the entopsychic processes that maintain the negative cognitive-behavioral orientation of drug abuse. Only through helping the client to develop an understanding of the mechanisms and processes that prevent him or her from expressing needs and problems in an appropriate manner can the therapist succeed in assisting the client to achieve disengagement from the world of drug abuse. From this basic therapeutic premise, it follows that the client must learn or relearn those social/emotional skills essential for living in traditional society, where drug abuse is incompatible with a healthy life.

The following case study depicts a client attempting to understand the entopsychic processes that have sparked his drug-abusing behavior.

The Case of W.F.   W.F. is a 31-year-old Caucasian male who is currently seeking readmission into a local drug detoxification and counseling center. His goals are twofold. He desires assistance in abstaining from abusing narcotics, as well as in "unraveling" his interpersonal problems, two conditions he believes are directly related to one another. In the past, W.F. has been treated with methadone for his drug addiction; he also received intensive, drug-free counseling for a period of two years before terminating his treatment.

This client reports that he has begun to experience increased levels of anxiety, fear, anger, frustration, and stress, conditions to which he has responded by using increasing amounts of Ts and Bs (a combination of Talwin and antihistamine), a behavior pattern that, he insists, relieves his "internal conflicts."

He further reports living in a common-law relationship for the past three years. He says, however, that he is unhappy with this arrangement and intends to terminate his relationship because he believes it contributes to his drug problems.

W.F. also indicates that he wants to live by himself until he can work through what he calls his "intrapsychic" problems. He is currently employed and is determined to maintain this employment, regardless of his present situation. This client is completely aware of his pattern of self-destructive behavior and/or its level of contribution to his drug abuse problems. Recently, he has become concerned about his own mental health.

Developing Understanding. As done previously (see Fig. 1.3), circles can be used to illustrate the dynamics of the macropsychosocial concepts under discussion. In Figure 1.5, three circles represent (1) the Declatypes, (2) the entopsychic processes, and

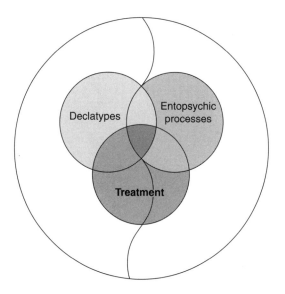

**FIGURE 1.5 Macropsychosocial Model
Illustrating the Concepts of Declatypes,
Entopsychic Processes, and Treatment Variables**

(3) the therapeutic, or treatment, process. Each circle can be seen as a variable operating within the dynamic system of the personality (larger white circle) and moving away from or toward the others, depending on the relative importance of each of the three variables. The circles/variables are in constant and fluid motion, their size and significance changing over time. As shown symbolically, dynamic interplay (overlapping) of the three variables is necessary for therapy to be effective. The area where the three inner circles overlap may be thought of as the area where an understanding of the needs and problems creating the drug-abusing behavior occurs and, in effect, a positive behavior orientation (PBO) occurs.

Whenever the variable of entopsychic processes (darker circle) shifts away from—to the right or left of—the other two circles so there is no overlap, no understanding by the addict of his or her drug-abusing behavior can take place. The model displayed in Figure 1.6 illustrates this sort of (failed) dynamic. Here, the Declatypical, or adverse, patterns of behavior adopted by the client obviously play a major contributory role in his or her inability to understand actual, realistic needs and problems.

Developing Self-Control. As mentioned in the Introduction to this book, essential to DECLARE Therapy are two attitudinal conceptualizations, or modalities: the negative behavioral orientation, or NBO, and the positive behavioral orientation, or PBO. The NBO is characteristic of the chronic, self-destructive nature of the drug abuser, who generally lacks sufficient motivation to recognize and accept the effects that continued substance abuse has on an individual's life (Taylor, 1988b). An NBO gives rise

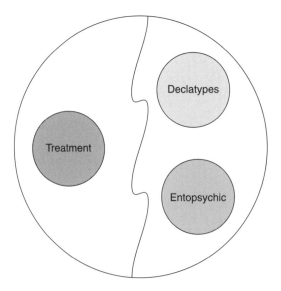

**FIGURE 1.6 Macropsychosocial Model
Illustrating a Lack of Understanding of Drug-
Abusing Behaviors**

to dwelling on negative thoughts, feelings, plans, intentions, failures, frustrations, and fears. To make matters worse, these negative thoughts generally lead to a self-fulfilling prophecy of continued, compulsive, noncontrolled drug-taking behavior despite its adverse consequences. The success of DECLARE Therapy hinges, in large part, on the substance abuser giving up his or her NBO.

In DECLARE Therapy, it is essential that the clinician assist the substance abuser in seeing himself or herself as more than an object being pushed around by uncontrollable forces. In essence, the clinician seeks to foster in the client a PBO, one based on mediated self-control and overt awareness of his or her drug-abusing behavior.

A PBO also encourages the client to direct his or her actions toward achieving some specific set of goals leading to cessation of substance abuse and to reestablishing proprietorship (internal loci of control) of personal thoughts and behaviors. Ideally, these efforts will enable the client to pursue opportunities that make his or her hopes and dreams concrete realities.

Positive Declatypes. The positive Declatypes of DECLARE Therapy refer to the biopsychosocial modalities that derive from the development of a PBO on the part of the substance abuser and, as noted earlier, fill out the DECLARE acronym (see earlier discussions in the Introduction and the section in this chapter on Developing Self-Control). To summarize here, the adoption of a PBO initiates a threefold process, according to which the abuser accepts the reality of his or her dependency on drugs (Declatype of Acceptance), which in turn enables the abuser to resolve to seek treatment (Declatype of Resolution) and eventually return to society (Declatype of re-Entry) as a viable member, free of the shackles of chemical dependency.

Basic Orientation Configuration Model. In DECLARE Therapy, the dynamic process of positive and negative behavioral orientation is graphically depicted by the Behavioral Orientation Configuration (BOC) Model (Fig. 1.7). First, the BOC Model depicts the decision on the part of an individual to use a drug or drugs and then move on to drug abuse, after passing through a period of sensitivity (to the drug). The individual is now set for a substance-related disorder. Once at the junction (i.e., at the bottom of the "V") the substance abuser must then decide or make a *declaration* to continue his or her journey.

If the abuser decides to proceed toward a PBO, then he or she will not develop a substance-related disorder and can enter society as a chemically free individual. Should the abuser decide to go toward an NBO, then he or she moves into the critical period zone, where the risk of developing the substance-related disorder increases. From this junction, the drug abuser moves into the Valley of Tears Syndrome (Taylor, 1988) and develops a substance-related disorder.

Determining an individual's behavioral orientation is crucial to the success of DECLARE Therapy, for it is only after a PBO or NBO has been established that an efficient and potentially effective plan for treatment can be initiated. In effect, it is the NBO and PBO that provide a focus for therapy, helping the client to develop an awareness of testing behavior. They also provide opportunities for feedback.

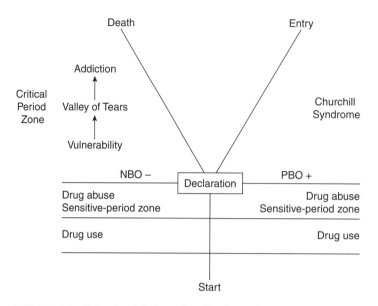

FIGURE 1.7   Behavioral Orientation Configuration Model

The clinician determines the behavioral orientation of a client simply by asking about personal activities (see Chapter 4). Once the orientation has been established, the client may be counseled about behaviors that may appear during treatment and that could potentially prevent positive growth and emotional stability—in other words, that prevent a movement toward empowerment.

When a client is made aware that others in therapy have experienced similar roadblocks to recovery, he or she may be better able to cope if and when these begin to appear. Adequately warned, the client is in a better position to avoid the feelings of inadequacy, inferiority, and isolation that frequently occur and to continue on the road to recovery.

The Decladine.   Finally, a diagram called the Decladine serves to demonstrate how the basic concepts of DECLARE Therapy work within a pre-treatment/post-treatment context (Fig. 1.8). According to this schema, pre-treatment places greater emphasis on the (biopsychosocial) assessment and diagnostic processes, less upon the Entry process. In post-treatment, this dynamic is reversed—that is, greater emphasis is placed on the Entry/aftercare (psychosocial) processes and less on the assessment and diagnostic processes.

Metapsychological Perspective

Researchers have found that recovering persons have statistically greater levels of faith and spirituality than those continuing to relapse. Also, those relapsing show sig-

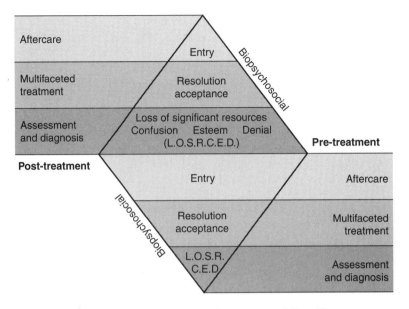

FIGURE 1.8   Decladine Illustrating Pre-Treatment and Post-Treatment Dynamics

nificantly lower levels of spirituality than those in recovery (Miller, 1991; Jarusiewicz, 2000; Johnson, 1993; Whitfield, 1984; Whitfield, 1985; Zinnbauer and Pargament, 2000; Sperry, 2001; Warfield and Goldstein, 1996). Inherent in both the development of and the belief in the effectiveness of DECLARE Therapy is the acceptance of the crucial element of spirituality in the healing process.

To understand the role of spirituality in recovery within the DECLARE therapeutic model, let's go back to the concept of the Valley of Tears. The journey into the Valley of Tears can result in a death sentence—unless the substance abuser can muster inner strength or undergo a transcendental experience.

Spirituality embraces the sides of both the darkness and the light of being—the experience of being lost and of being found. Moving out of the Valley of Tears is a human journey, one taking a lonely soul from the trauma of pain, of being stuck and addicted, to the liberating and exhilarating state of becoming free. Symbolically, it is a journey out of the barren desert into the richness and fullness of life.

The Churchill Syndrome.   DECLARE Therapy embraces this sense of spirituality—of being in the desert and lost and of finding new life—and calls it the Churchill Syndrome (Taylor, 1988b).

As history tells us, Britain's prime minister Winston Churchill (himself an alcoholic, by the way) embarked on a journey that resulted in an astounding victory. In leading his people during the bombings of World War II, he stood as a symbol of victory over the invading Germans. From the beginning, his was an uphill climb in the face of insurmountable odds. Certainly his inner spirit played a role in his determination to fight.

Just as Churchill was victorious, chemically dependent individuals can triumph over the biopsychosocial onslaught of psychoactive drugs. Symbolic of this experience is the letter **V,** the configuration of which, as we saw in the Basic Configuration Model (see Fig. 1.7), effectively describes the twofold thrust of the syndrome's journey. Using the configuration once again, Figure 1.9 demonstrates the relationship of the Churchill Syndrome to the seven basic DECLARE modalities.

On the negative side (descending slope) of the **V** configuration are those modalities inhibiting successful intervention into the process of substance use disorders—that is, the negative Declatypes. Thus, the descending slope represents the chronic, self-destructive behavior of the drug abuser who is without sufficient motivation either to recognize or to accept the adverse consequences of continued drug abuse.

Clients displaying the behavior of the descending-slope configuration run a greater risk of developing poor health, psychological disorders, physiological disorders, emotional disorders, and possibly death from prolonged drug abuse. The modalities that inhibit successful intervention and/or block acceptance are Denial, Esteem, Confusion, and Loss of Significant Resources.

On the positive side (ascending slope) of the **V** configuration are those traits that enhance the drug abuser's chances of successfully recovering from the effects of substance-related disorders—that is, the positive Declatypes. This ascending slope signifies overt awareness and acceptance of the destructive aspects of drug abuse, crucial to beginning the process of empowerment, whereby the individual is highly motivated (by a variety of internal and external resources) to abstain from abusive, drug-taking behavior. In its proposition of the Declatypes of Acceptance, Resolution, and Entry and an ascending slope to the striving of its clients, DECLARE Therapy represents, in effect, an optimistic approach to the treatment of substance-related disorders. The belief in a successful outcome can indeed be a self-fulfilling prophecy—a positive one.

V for Victory.   Translated to the metapsychological plane, the Churchill Syndrome is a concept that serves to conceptualize the spiritual experience of the client. Again, the letter **V** is an effective symbol of this transcendent experience.

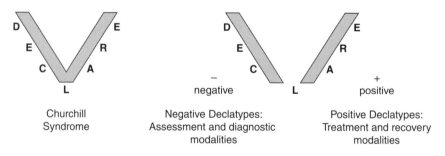

FIGURE 1.9   Drug Dependency Tread Configuration

(Modified from Taylor, 1988b. Courtesy of Charles C. Thomas, Publisher, Springfield, Illinois.)

The syndrome focuses on a person's need to surrender to the inner world of the soul and to accept the strength available through the human spirit. The experience is at once a universal and highly personal one. Transcending all boundaries, the positive experience of the Churchill Syndrome is ecumenical in nature and, consequently, reinforces any religious or philosophical beliefs (Christianity, Judaism, Muslimism, Buddhism, etc.) the client may hold. At the same time, the details of each individual's experience are unique.

Ironically, the client's first step toward experiencing the lifelong healing that comes with the integration of spirituality into day-to-day life is admitting that he or she has become powerless over the effect of alcohol/drug addiction—that life has become confused and unmanageable. Only after the individual recognizes and accepts this state of affairs can the Churchill Syndrome be experienced and the journey begun. Tapping into the human spirit, the wounded or injured wayfarer embarks on what will probably be the most significant adventure of his or her life. When the Churchill Syndrome is used positively by the client, it leads to the ultimate goal: victory over addiction. The byproduct, hope, helps in reclaiming a gift that is ours by our very birthright—the wholeness and richness of life.

An Entopsychic Journey into Wholeness. One of the basic, and most crucial, goals of therapy is to assist the client through his or her journey to wholeness. To become a fully functioning, well-integrated person, an individual must know himself or herself as completely as possible. Certainly, a person who remains totally oblivious to his or her true self and to the surrounding world cannot become whole.

In DECLARE Therapy, the developmental process of the client's PBO toward personal wholeness is conceived essentially as an inner one, whence the term *entopsychic,* from the Greek *entos,* meaning "within." Ultimately the goal of therapy is to help the client do battle with the demons of unconsciousness within, to come to terms with them, and to return eventually to society drug free and dedicated to achieving long-term quality sobriety.

Recapping . . .

■ The challenge of illicit drug abuse in our society must be answered with positive, proactive responses that persuade people not to abuse alcohol and other drugs in the first place.

■ Because it represents a nonlinear, multifaceted, cognitive-behavioral, proactive approach, DECLARE Therapy can be a viable and effective means to answering this challenge.

■ The DECLARE model views the client from three perspectives: micropsychological (including biopsychological and intrapersonal aspects), macropsychosocial, and metapsychological.

■ Declatypes refer to the patterns of behavior displayed by those who use mind-altering drugs despite adverse consequences.

■ DECLARE Therapy recognizes seven Declatypes (whence the acronym), four of which derive from a negative behavioral orientation (NBO), giving rise to the Declatypical syndromes of Denial, Esteem, Confusion, and Loss of Significant Resources, and three of which derive from a positive behavioral orientation (PBO) to produce the threefold process of Acceptance, Resolution, and Entry.

■ One of the therapist's major challenges is to assist the client in understanding the entopsychic processes that have given rise to the abusing behavior.

■ Essential to the therapeutic model is an acceptance of what the author has termed the Churchill Syndrome. Just as Winston Churchill drew on the inner strength of his human spirit to lead his people through the dark days of World War II's blitzkrieg, the abuser on the road to recovery must acknowledge spiritual reality and draw on it. No journey from hurting to wholeness can be accomplished without tapping into the amazing strength of the human spirit.

2 Basic Methods and Techniques

Without doubt, addiction is a most curious disease. Just consider . . .

Addictionologists have established that five out of every seven persons who use drugs abuse them (Talbott, 1982); one out of the five who abuse drugs will develop the disease of chemical dependency, but two out of the five will abuse more than the person who is diseased! What may explain these astonishing statistics is the multitude of factors contributing to the onset of the disease (Talbott, 1982; Taylor, 1988b).

As explained earlier in the text, chemical dependency can be viewed as involving an interaction of three constituent systems: (1) the biological, (2) the emotional-motivational, and (3) the social. Effective intervention for chemical dependency must deliberately take into account each of them. Likewise, chemical dependency counselors and mental health professionals who evaluate and treat substance use, abuse, and dependency require a flexible framework for organizing their interventions within each of these systems.

Until the advent of DECLARE Therapy, no such framework existed. Over the past several decades, a number of therapeutic approaches have been employed in attempting to understand the nature of both the physiological and psychological factors involved in the development of mental disorders. These therapies vary in their application to substance abuse disorders. Thus, drug abusers and those who are chemically dependent have traditionally been treated by therapeutic approaches that were not specifically designed for them (National Institute on Drug Abuse, 1992), so it was somewhat out of frustration that the DECLARE model was conceived, with the goal to develop a method of therapy designed specifically for the situations and needs of drug and alcohol *abuse* victims. Let's now take a closer look at the model, first examining its multifaceted nature and then specific procedural techniques used in the course of treatment, included the pivotally important Modality Profile.

A Multifaceted Approach

In the creation of the treatment plan, it is important for the clinician/therapist to keep in mind that drug abusers represent a wide diversity of individuals. They are of both sexes and represent various ethnic groups, races, and ages. They come from different socio-economic backgrounds and have different psychological characteristics. They are drug dependent in different ways and to varying degrees. They use drugs to meet different needs (Brill, 1981). Obviously, if we are to expect any measure of success, it is necessary to develop a treatment approach that understands and responds to this diversity.

As emphasized throughout this text, the strength of DECLARE Therapy lies in its unique approach, one that aids the therapist in assisting the drug abuser to view the disease of chemical dependency from the perspective of seven specific modalities and that provides a multifaceted approach for identifying needs related to:

- Psychological profile
- Physiological makeup
- Social environment
- Cultural background
- Gender-specific concerns
- Counseling services
- Individual and group treatments
- Use of chemotherapeutic agents in treatment
- Daycare
- Birth control
- Pregnancy counseling
- Education

As we look at therapeutic methods and techniques in some detail, it is important to keep in mind the fact that the use of any therapeutic technique demands flexibility, sensitivity, timing, professional knowledge, and clinical intuition (Meichenbaum, 1977). The therapist must apply a systematic approach to problem solving; combat globalizing, catastrophizing, and all-or-nothing thinking (Eimer, 1988); and select therapeutic techniques based on an analysis of the problems identified and targeted for intervention in the drug abuser's Modality Profile (Lazarus, 1985b; Eimer, 1988).

Historically, frontline chemical dependency professionals have not integrated medical psychotherapeutic techniques into their armamentarium. In its methodological approach, this text relies heavily on the definition proposed by Pruzensky (1988) that medical psychotherapy is a hybrid discipline composed of many subdisciplines, including:

- Consultation-liaison psychiatry
- Clinical psychiatry
- Nursing
- Pediatric psychology
- Medical psychology
- Health psychology and counseling
- Behavioral health

Medical psychotherapists typically apply knowledge of personality functioning and change to highly specialized areas of medicine, thus facilitating prevention, rehabilitation, and provision of direct services. The multifaceted approach offered by DECLARE

Therapy represents a synthesis of the practice of medical psychotherapy with cognitive behavioral practices.

DECLARE Therapy may be used in treating children, adolescents, adults, couples, families, and/or groups. Because of its comprehensive approach, it may also be effective in dealing with:

- Sexual perpetrators
- Victims of sexual abuse
- Battered women
- Perpetrators of abuse
- Grief victims
- Clients dealing with codependency and other relationship problems
- Individuals suffering from addictions of any kind (food, gambling, sex, etc.)

However, therapists should be cautious in utilizing any model to treat disorders that are outside their scope of practice or knowledge.

Modality Profile

Effective psychotherapy with persons experiencing substance-related disorders requires that they be assessed in each of the seven modalities for deficiencies, negative and/or positive symptoms, and disruptions. Within the first few sessions, a Modality Profile should be completed. This step is critical, for the profile can, then, serve as a guide for setting treatment goals (Taylor, 1988b).

As noted earlier, the construction of a Modality Profile is a method popularized by Arnold Lazarus and used in DECLARE Therapy for listing and systematically organizing the issues and problems to be targeted for intervention. This profile facilitates the adaptation and fitting of psychotherapy to the client's unique needs (Lazarus, 1985a, 1985b, 1981). (See Figure 0.1, page xix, and discussion in Chapter 4).

It is important to keep in mind that the individual modalities are not mutually exclusive, although the categories are distinct conceptually and problems are sometimes listed under more than one modality. Nevertheless, therapeutic interventions are organized to target specific problems listed under individual modalities.

Obviously, the choice of techniques or approaches to be used should follow logically and systematically from the assessment data obtained from the client. DECLARE Therapy uses the following four instruments:

1. A structured interview entitled the Taylor Historical Questionnaire-Revised (THQ-R) (Taylor, 1988d)
2. Multifaceted Assessment of Chemical Dependency Inventory-Revised (MAC-D-R) (Taylor, 1988a)
3. Biphasic Analysis Reintegration Sequence (BARS) (1988c)
4. The Taylor Draw-A-Person-In-The-Rain Anxiety Scale-Revised (DAPIR-R) (contact author for test)

Other instruments of use to the clinician (but not essential to the assessment and diagnostic process unless dual disorders are suspected) include:

- Neuropsychological screening tests (Lezak, 1983)
- Paper/pencil tests
- Alcohol and drug inventories
- Minnesota Multiphasic Personality Inventories (MMPI, MMPI-2, MMPI-A) (Graham, 1990; Green, 1980)
- McAndrews Scales (Hathaway and McKinley, 1943)
- The Rorschach (1921) (Lezak, 1983; Matsunaga, 1983)
- Bender Visual Motor Gestalt Test 20 (Bender, 1978; Lubin et al., 1986)
- Beck Depression Scale (Beck, 1982)
- Wechsler Adult Intelligence Scale–Revised (Wechsler, 1981)

These tests should, of course, be administered only by those professionals qualified to do so. Clinicians are further cautioned that should they decide to use the instruments listed above, it is usually appropriate to wait ten days to two weeks after detoxification before administering these tests. In some instances, additional time may be needed.

The specific categories of data that should be collected in an initial multifaceted assessment include the following information concerning the client and his or her situation:

- Medical and psychiatric histories
- Family demographics and history
- Current living situation
- Recreational preferences
- Precipitating events
- Circumstances of drug abuse onset
- Specific characteristics of substance abuse
- Course of substance abuse over time
- Effects of situations and activities on substance abuse
- Psychological and physiological complaints

Also important is the gathering of information concerning (1) the client's personal constructs of why he or she abuses drugs and what personal meanings are assigned to the abused chemicals and (2) the way(s) in which the client has coped with his or her substance-abusing behavior and how this behavior has affected various areas of day-to-day living: interpersonal relationships, medical status, family and social dealings, work, finances, and so forth.

The initial assessment centers on two basic questions the clinician must ask of the client:

1. How hard are you willing to work on changing your negative behavior(s)?
2. What expectations do you have concerning how your life will be different after your substance-abusing behavior has been arrested?

Of course, a thorough, multifaceted assessment is composed of numerous questions. The next section presents an extensive list of specific questions clinicians may use in building a Modality Profile. (See Chapters 3 and 4 for further discussion of the assessment process.)

Procedural Questions

Questions for the Clinician
- What is getting in the way of the client accepting that there is a drug abuse problem?
- What is the client's mood? His/her feelings?
- How does the client's method of avoidance, indifference, and/or evasiveness manifest itself?
- In what methods does the client engage to blame others concerning the problem(s)?
- What are other people doing to the client's life?
- What is the client doing to other individuals' lives?
- What ongoing plans does the client have regarding his/her drug abuse behavior?
- Does the client have any fears regarding confidentiality?

Questions for the Client Self-Worth and Self-Image
- What makes you feel a lack of self-worth?
- What happens when you have these feelings?
- How do you behave when you have these feelings?
- Do you blame yourself for your current problems?
- What happens when you lose self-respect?
- What would happen if someone disapproved of and/or rejected you?
- What happens when you become angry?
- How do you view yourself?
- Do you like who you are?
- How often do you experience depression? guilt? shame?
- How would you describe your self-image?
- What are your best assets?
- Name five of your most positive qualities.

Questions for the Client Concerning Use and Abuse of Drugs
- What happens when you lose control of your drinking/drugging?
- How often have you experienced loss of memory during drug use?
- How many times have you been involved in traffic violations?
- What are your feelings before you drink or drug?
- Have you ever experienced feelings of depression or anxiety whenever you could not use?
- How did you feel when you were arrested for the first time?
- Have you ever been hurt or injured when you were under the influence of alcohol or drugs?

- Have you ever hurt or injured someone when you were drinking or drugging?
- What was confinement like? What did you do?
- How did your family feel?

Questions for the Client Concerning Health and Values
- How is your present state of health?
- How is your sex life?
- How are things on the job?
- What present difficulties are you experiencing?
- How long have you been on parole, probation or furlough?
- How many friends do you have?
- What psychological problems are you currently experiencing?
- What are your current sources of income?
- How do your thoughts affect your behavior?
- Who are the most important persons in your life?
- What do you believe other people want from you?

Questions for the Client Concerning Goals
- What caused you to seek treatment at this time?
- What are your current feelings regarding the use/abuse of drugs?
- What would you like to do more of?
- What would you like to do less of?
- What do you plan to do with your life in the near future?
- What would happen if you were unable to receive treatment?
- What do you believe treatment should do?
- What special expectations do you have?

Questions for the Client Concerning Expectations
- What do you expect from treatment?
- How long do you think therapy should take?
- What level of commitment are you willing to give?
- Do you believe there is any hope for you?
- What are your strong points?
- How will you live without drugs/alcohol?
- What are your goals?

Questions Concerning Client's Everyday Life and Future
- What are your present fears?
- Who is your support person?
- What are your living arrangements?
- Do you have a job?
- What are your sources of income?
- Who are your friends?
- What are your current legal problems?
- How will you make it in your new world?

- What problems do you foresee?
- How will you recognize these problems?
- What will you do when these "warning signs" appear?
- How will you monitor yourself?

Once the assessment has been conducted, the client should be socialized according to the DECLARE therapeutic approach.

Personal Socialization Process

Beginning with the initial contact, the client should be socialized to the conceptual framework of self-management through the effective utilization of coping skills. The socialization process includes discussion of drug use as a complex, multifaceted phenomenon.

The therapist, for instance, informs the client that substance-related disorders are experienced in many different, interactive modalities. This approach is advantageous, for it emphasizes the many windows of entry for coping with substance abuse and for ameliorating it.

According to the client's perspective, the management of substance-related disorders is conceptualized as a set of skills, and the idea is presented to the client that he or she may have more of an ability for refining some skills than others. In addition, as strengths in one modality increase, they may compensate for weaknesses in others.

It is also important for the client to develop a clear understanding of both the treatment plan and the critical nature of the Modality Profile, a tool that provides the therapist with the key to staying on task and remaining focused on appropriate and workable treatment goals (see Chapter 4). Although this profile provides a holistic picture, the key to therapeutic success is for the clinician/therapist/counselor to *model* for the client how to take global problems and break them down into manageable units.

The Modality Profile is effectively organized for this purpose. By tracing the client's progress with the profile, the therapist is able to note each small success in resolving specific problems within a given modality. These small changes accumulate and, gradually, alter the total picture for the chemically dependent individual.

Each client presents the therapist with unique therapeutic challenges. The work is often quite difficult and requires a high degree of empathy on the part of the professional counselor. The potential benefits, however, are extremely rewarding.

Detoxification

As you might have already assumed, DECLARE Therapy is an appropriate and effective treatment on both an outpatient and inpatient basis. It can be effectively incorporated into an inpatient setting using a triphasic process of detoxification.

The first phase of the detoxification process is complete abstinence from all types of psychoactive drugs. The only medications permitted are those needed to sustain life. During this phase, biological/medical intervention may be required—for example, enzyme multiplied immunoassay test (EMIT), high-pressure liquid chromatography (HPLC), gas chromatography (GC), blood levels, and/or the use of a known intoxicant or an antagonist. At this stage, in the DECLARE approach, it has been found helpful to point out to the client, in a nonthreatening manner, something about the physical symptoms encountered during the detoxification process (see flowchart, Figure 2.1).

The second phase of the detoxification process addresses the physiological, physiotherapeutic, and recreational treatment needs of the client, including:

- A balanced nutritional diet at fixed intervals (three times a day)
- Food supplements
- Exercise consisting of walking, jogging
- Massages to dissipate muscular cramping

The third phase of the detoxification process emphasizes the client's need for psychological and emotional support.

After completing the triphasic detoxification process, the client is introduced to the DECLARE approach to treatment. Issues and problems in the Modality Profile should be identified by both the therapist and the client in terms of their urgency and priority. The issues identified must also be defined in concrete cognitive and behavioral terms, and (as previously mentioned) global complaints should be made specific by breaking them down into their component parts, thus preventing them from becoming overwhelming. With this in mind, let's take a look at a number of techniques that can be useful in assisting the client to achieve victory over chemical dependency.

Procedural Techniques

Personal Surgery Technique

Ask clients to imagine that they are surgeons. Then instruct them to closely examine themselves in an effort to discover the truth about their thoughts and behaviors—much as a surgeon would operate on a patient to discover the cause of a particular condition or disease.

Clients should be asked to "cut deeply" under the surface and to expose the faults, failures, shortcomings, and feelings that are producing the substance-abusing behaviors (negative thoughts, personal style, perceptions, emotions, sense of self, motivation, behavior, and interpersonal functioning), that is, the NBO.

Clients must operate on aspects of their lives as skillfully as does a surgeon who performs a delicate operation, and just as surgeons are confident and fearless as they

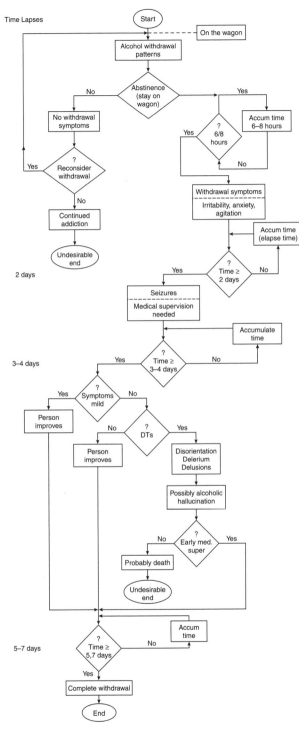

In alcohol withdrawal, withdrawal patterns will begin as soon as the decision to remain abstinent is made. If abstinence is not chosen, no withdrawal patterns will be noted, unless withdrawal is reconsidered at a later time. If abstinence is not reconsidered, continued addiction will lead to no further withdrawal patterns and an undesirable termination. Once abstinence is chosen, the first withdrawal symptoms will appear in approximately six to eight hours. These symptoms include irritability, anxiety, and agitation. As time goes by, the symptoms of the first stage of withdrawal may reoccur before the next stage is reached, or the subject may go directly into the next stage. This cycle of reoccurring symptoms may continue for as long as two days before the second stage of symptoms appears. Seizures (which require medical supervision) are the second stage of alcohol withdrawal. The subject may have mild symptoms which lead to a general improvement and a complete withdrawal with a favorable end. If the symptoms are not mild, then the subject will continue to the DT stage. If the subject does experience DTs, then the next stage—including disorientation, delirium, and delusions—will lead directly to possible alcoholic hallucinations before complete withdrawal and a favorable termination. If the subject does experience DTs, then early medical supervision should be obtained to bring the subject into complete withdrawal and a favorable termination. If early medical supervision is not obtained, then death will probably result.

FIGURE 2.1   Flowchart of Alcohol Withdrawal Patterns

(Modified from Taylor, 1988b. Courtesy of Charles C. Thomas, Publisher, Springfield, Illinois.)

31

cut through their patients' tissue, addicts and alcoholics must likewise be fearless in uncovering the sources of their disease process—for example, anger, resentment, fears, anxieties, insecurities, loneliness, isolation, abandonment, ambitions, sexual relations, low self-esteem.

Some surgeries may not require as much time as others, but the results will be the same: wellness. So it is with addicts, who must "cut away" the layers that bind them to the disease of chemical dependency. After these layers have been cut away, the "incision" can be closed and the healing process begun.

This is not to suggest that scars will not form. Of course they will, but with the proper care and with time, they will become less noticeable.

Stress Reduction

Stress reduction techniques encourage clients to identify the sources of stress in their daily lives, to note the specific ways they experience stress and to develop strategies for reducing it (Nash, 1976). In DECLARE Therapy, the client is encouraged to keep a daily log of thoughts and feelings.

Thoughts, in fact, are quite significant in stress reduction, as negative thoughts contribute to emotional and psychological wear and tear. In a stressful situation, negative thoughts can exacerbate the deleterious effects of stress on the body. The following instructions and questions (adapted from Nash, 1976) may be used to assist the client in developing a journal or a daily log:

- Notice when you need the drug.
- Where are you feeling the discomfort? Describe the discomfort.
- Notice your surroundings. Where are you?
- Is anyone with you? Who?
- What's going on while you're experiencing the discomfort?
- What's your first response to the discomfort? What do you want to do? Do you want to take a drug or escape your surroundings?
- What do you finally do?

DAPIR Anxiety Scale-Revised

The Taylor Draw-A-Person-In-The-Rain Anxiety Scale-Revised (DAPIR-R) is a method that assesses the level of anxiety being experienced by the client. Like the Kinetic Family Drawing, it is simple to implement. The subject is given an 8½- by 11-inch sheet of unlined, white bond paper and a sharpened, no. 2 pencil with eraser and is asked to "Draw a person in the rain."

A scoring manual designed by the author to assess anxiety has been created so that the indices may be scored by 1, 2, 3, 4, or 5. A table of norms and T-score values, percentiles, means and standard deviations, reliabilities, and a psychogram are provided for the clinician to determine the level of anxiety in the client. (Contact author.)

The Empty Chair Technique

DECLARE Therapy uses an adaptation of the Empty Chair technique popularized by Frederick Perls in his Gestalt Therapy (Perls, Hefferline, and Goodman, 1951). The object of Perls's technique was to help an individual get in touch with the part(s) of the self that had not previously been integrated into the whole person. Accordingly in DECLARE Therapy, clients' internalized object relations are played out with the drug of choice.

In the DECLARE model, the therapist has the client enter into a dialogue with the drug in an empty chair, encouraging the client to role-play both sides of the conscious/unconscious split in personality while sitting in the chairs (which are facing each other). The instructions may sound something like this:

—Your drug is sitting in that chair opposite you. Please sit in that chair now and give your drug a voice. Speak for the drug, to yourself, in the chair you just left.

Whenever significant experiences occur in the role of the drug, the client is asked to switch chairs and speak for himself or herself *to* the drug. The client is encouraged to continue to alternate roles until some important integrations take place. At this point, the therapist may interject a comment such as, "You mean you are very angry and you want to kick the habit?"

Self-Hypnosis

Self-hypnosis and guided imagery are useful techniques that can be taught to the drug abuser in a skill-based program created to alter perceptions and images. In reality, the therapeutic use of self-hypnosis with chemically dependent clients depends on the acquisition and reinforcement of several skills:

- Focusing attention
- Generating vivid images
- Inducing a state of relaxed wakefulness (Kroger & Fezler, 1976)

The hypnotic techniques outlined by Kroger and Fezler for the treatment of drug abuse are based on repeatedly emphasizing, under hypnosis:

- The deleterious effects of drugs
- The client's ability to control his or her own behavior
- The importance of recognizing the emotional needs for the symptoms

Ideally, the self-destructive drives should be channeled into healthy activities that involve concentration and balance—things like swimming, jogging, biking, and so forth. The client should also be encouraged to participate in other sports, hobbies, and social activities.

Guided Imagery

Guided imagery is a technique that puts clients in touch with internal processes outside of their awareness. In other words, therapists and their clients are able to harness the power of the imagination to evoke specific physiological changes as an aid to therapy. Currently a number of clinicians are experimenting with the creative use of mental imagery in behavior rehearsal, dream-drama, and other techniques.

The first step in imagery techniques is relaxation. Several methods, used singly or jointly, can help the client achieve this desirable state: meditation; progressive relaxation of the body's muscles from head to toe; focusing on one's breathing while allowing all other thoughts to slip away; or by recalling some pleasant setting.

Imaging itself stimulates the body to relax and inhibits muscle activity as well as verbal thoughts, whereupon mental images become dominant. The therapist composes a scene that seems to capture the client's conflicts, fears, and/or desires for change (Bernstein and Borkover, 1975).

In using guided imagery, the therapist requires that the client project himself/ herself into the scene and then describe it aloud. Usually, the therapist selects something or someone alive in that scene (other than the client) and then directs the client to "get in touch" with this "inner adviser" (Sherman and Fredman, 1986). This technique can be used whenever the client is experiencing trouble with the way he or she is handling a situation or making a choice or plan. The therapist has the "adviser" take the drug-abusing behavior away from the client while seeking his or her agreement to do so. Finally, the therapist directs the client to return to his or her usual state from the relaxed one.

Life Boat Fantasy Technique

The Life Boat Fantasy technique, which was influenced by Lazarus's Deserted Island Fantasy technique (Lazarus, 1981), facilitates the therapist's endeavor to understand the inner world of the addict. This technique is especially useful when the rationale of the client for abusing drugs resists analysis and remains obscure.

The following is an example of how to talk with the client in administering the technique:

> —Please sit back and relax. I would like to ask your cooperation and indulgence during this fantasy experience. Try to use your imagination to its fullest. Attempt to engage yourself directly with the situation that I am about to describe to you. Try hard to imagine how you think you might react if you were really in this situation.

> —Now . . . imagine that you are being magically transported to the middle of the ocean, where you will be placed in a life boat in which you will be forced to remain for a period of eight weeks. Due to a lack of options, nothing you say or do will prevent your being transported. Can you picture this? If you can visualize this occurrence, please raise your index finger on either hand.

—Before you are transported, certain information is provided to you. You are told that while you are in the life boat, the rest of the world outside this office will remain in suspended animation—that is, time will stand still while you live, day after day, week after week, in your life boat. You are also told that the boat is filled with alcohol and drugs and drug paraphernalia for your use. When you reappear back in this office, you will see that the date is the exact date on which you were initially transported.

—It is also important to note that you may choose company or solitude before being transported—that is, you may choose to spend eight weeks in the life boat with a pleasant person of the opposite sex *(when dealing with a homosexual, a person of the same sex)* waiting for you in the life boat. This is a person whom you have not met before. Some people are happy to spend eight weeks in their own company, with their own thoughts, in peace and solitude. Other individuals, however, definitely want company—even though they have never met their life boat companion. Now, please choose solitude or companionship. Now when you have made your choice, raise your index finger on either hand. After the choice is made, the fantasy will begin.

—Now that you have made your choice, you are being transported and will soon appear in the life boat. If you can picture this, please indicate by raising your index finger on either hand. If you have chosen a companion, that person welcomes you to the life boat. He/she is pleasant, attractive, warm, and friendly. Now please answer the following questions.

   (1) If you have chosen a companion to accompany you: What are you thinking about? How are events unfolding as they are actually occurring? How do you get along with your life boat companion? Given these questions, what do you think might go wrong? How much self-disclosure will you exercise with your companion? What type of relationship will you have with your companion? How will things turn out? (2) If you have chosen solitude: What does it feel like to be alone? What will you focus your thoughts on? Are you happy or unhappy with your solitude?

While the Life Boat technique should be employed during the first several sessions, it can be effectively used at anytime during therapy. The precise wording used in administering the technique may, of course, be altered to suit the age, intelligence, personality, and particular circumstances of the client.

Self-Monitoring: BARS

Self-monitoring is an important method that requires the addict to employ specific types of record keeping—of thoughts, feelings, and behavior—to heighten the client's awareness of the drug-abusing behavior. The preferred method of reporting signs of the addict's NBO is the use of the Biphasic Analysis Reintegration Sequence (BARS).

   BARS is a self-monitoring technique employed during the entry/reentry phase of drug treatment whereby the client monitors daily activities so as to remain chemically free. The client is asked to keep a daily record of any warning signs that may indicate relapse.

Whenever such warning signals occur, the client must record them on the daily record sheet and indicate what action was taken to handle the situation. The client must also rate each day and week on a scale of 1 to 10, with 1 representing "poor," 5 representing "moderate," and 10 representing "optimal."

In addition, the client is asked to take a few minutes daily, at bedtime, to select five (non-drug-related) activities (reinforcement menu) that gives him or her pleasure and plan to enjoy the activities the next day, after which they are reported on the daily record.

Taylor Historical Questionnaire-Revised

The Taylor Historical Questionnaire-Revised (THQ-R) is a structured interview questionnaire designed to assess the client's alcohol and substance abuse history by using the DECLARE acronym. The client is asked to complete the questionnaire at home after the first session and to bring it back to the second session. The clinician may also use the THQ-R as part of a structured interview by asking questions directly from the questionnaire. Upon receiving the information from the THQ-R, the clinician should review the questionnaire and clear up any misconceptions prior to developing, with the client, an initial Modality Profile and treatment plan. (See also the section on THQ-R Assessment in Chapter 3.)

The MAC-D-R

The Multifaceted Assessment of Chemical Dependency Inventory–Revised (MAC-D-R) is a clinician's worksheet and guide for use in conceptualizing multifaceted determinants of problems and issues in the treatment planning of substance-related disorders.

The form facilitates a thorough assessment across all seven DECLARE modalities, thus encouraging systematic treatment planning and evaluation of the client. The MAC-D-R is an instrument designed to provide the clinician with a diagram for processing and evaluating data provided by the client. All information on the MAC-D-R may be modified, expanded, or updated by the clinician to reflect the current stage of therapy. In addition, relevant information gathered from other drug and alcohol assessment instruments, inventories, interviews, psychological tests, and observations may also be recorded on the form. The MAC-D-R also provides a guide for assessing mental status, suicide lethality, and violence potential. For further discussion of this assessment tool, see Using the MAC-D-R in Chapter 4.

Thought-Stopping

Thought-stopping is an effective technique for combating obsessive and intrusive thoughts about drugs. This technique requires the client to subvocally scream, "STOP!"

over and over again. It is often helpful to suggest that the client think of a large light that is flashing the word "stop" on and off.

One DECLARE Therapy client, for instance, was encouraged to nonverbally say the word "stop" over and over again whenever she was obsessed with thoughts of using crack cocaine. Combining this thought-stopping technique with relaxation (a technique she had learned in a previous session), she was able to bring her thoughts under control.

Goal Rehearsal

This is a procedure that encourages the client to mentally rehearse a desired behavior. This could be considered a form of problem solving in advance. The practice of self-instruction can have positive outcomes and can increase the individual's sense of self-efficacy.

Diversion

Various diversion procedures have been designed to divert the client's attention away from drugs and toward something positive. One effective method is involvement in physical activities such as walking, jogging, swimming, or some other structured exercise program. Another technique is that of having the client carry three different objects in his or her pocket—for example, three coins (penny, nickel, quarter)—and to focus attention on identifying them whenever thoughts of drugs enter into consciousness. The client may also be encouraged to carry a symbol of something he or she has lost due to drug abuse—a photo or coin, for instance.

Time Projection

In the Time Projection technique, the client is asked to sit quietly and to imagine that he or she is somewhere in the future, six months or a year from the present time. While imagining this scenario, the client predicts what life will be like at this point. This technique provides a vehicle for discussion with the client about treatment and about the future.

Drug and Alcohol Education

The client is asked to read books and/or articles to facilitate progress in therapy. It should be emphasized that the reading be done carefully and that important points should be noted for future reference. To ascertain what (if any) impact the material has had on the client and to clarify ambiguities, client and therapist discuss the readings in subsequent therapy sessions.

Self-Esteem Exercise

The Self-Esteem Exercise is designed to contradict any internalized messages of worth-lessness and thereby replace them with positive-self-worth messages and healthy self-esteem. The client is asked to write ten positive statements about himself or herself—five concerning personality and five concerning accomplishments—with each statement beginning with "I." (The number of statements may be expanded, if desired.)

The client is then instructed to read the list aloud and the therapist gives an enthusiastically positive response, with constructive comments following the reading. The therapist should pay particular attention to whether or not the client uses qualifiers in his statements. The therapist should also look for signs of embarrassment and/or uncertainty about the statements and should encourage the client to repeat the list until he/she sounds convinced that the statements being vocalized are, indeed, true. This technique can also be quite effective in a group situation.

Write Your Drug Story Technique

In the Write Your Drug Story technique, the client is asked to write a story about his or her use of drugs and/or alcohol. The instructions are deliberately left open-ended and vague to see how the client perceives the dynamics of her dependency. As the client presents the information, she is encouraged to identify thoughts and feelings that accompany the various experiences. At this point the clinician asks the client various questions concerning what was written and what was said. The therapist, therefore, attempts to involve the client emotionally. This technique may also be used in a group setting.

Do I Hate You? Technique

In the Do I Hate You? technique, the client is asked to write a letter to the disease of chemical dependency, detailing how much he hates the disease. The client is then asked to read the letter aloud, after which his feelings regarding the hatred of the disease are discussed. This technique may assist the client in coping with denial and in separating illusion from reality.

Recapping . . .

■ The disease of chemical dependency is a unique one involving the interaction of three constituent systems: the biological, the emotional/motivational, and the social.

■ Professional counselors and therapists dealing with chemically dependent clients require a flexible framework for organizing their interventions within each of these systems, a framework designed specifically for assisting the client on his or her road to recovery.

■ Until the advent of DECLARE Therapy, no such framework existed.

■ DECLARE Therapy uses a nonlinear multifaceted approach wherein the therapist separates each of the client's problems into levels and then chooses an appropriate technique for each level. Within the DECLARE model, these levels include Denial, Esteem, Confusion, and Loss of Significant Resources.

■ DECLARE Therapy incorporates numerous techniques for addressing the major problems likely to be identified within each of the seven modalities of the DECLARE acronym.

■ The multifaceted causes of and problems associated with chemical dependency present therapists with unique therapeutic challenges. The work is often quite difficult and requires a high degree of empathy on the part of the professional counselor. The potential rewards, however, can be extremely gratifying.

3 The Initial Interview

Generally speaking, when it comes to conducting the initial interview, the DECLARE therapist has the same goals as most clinicians:

- Establish rapport with the client
- Assess and evaluate the presenting complaints
- Determine the best course of treatment

Beyond these goals, the DECLARE therapist is apt to follow some important points of departure, focusing on areas of concern specific to the seven therapeutic modalities. This chapter describes in detail the components of a sound initial interview.

Assessing the Client

Following are questions to be addressed during the initial interview, grouped according to the seven basic Declatypes.

Denial

- What is getting in the way of the client accepting that there is a drug/alcohol abuse problem?
- What are the client's mood and feelings?
- How do the clients' methods of avoidance/indifference/evasiveness manifest themselves?
- In what methods does the client engage to blame others concerning his/her problems?
- How are others influencing the client's life?
- How is the client affecting the lives of others?
- What ongoing plans does the client have regarding his/her drug-abusing behavior?

■ What are his/her excuses or reasons for using chemical substances?
■ How does the client minimize his/her drug use?

Esteem

■ How does the client view himself/herself?
■ What is the client's self-image?
■ Does the client approve of himself/herself?
■ What makes the client feel a loss of self-esteem?
■ What happens when the client experiences feelings of worthlessness?
■ Does the client blame himself/herself for the current situation?
■ How does the client behave when these feelings are experienced?
■ What happens when the client experiences a loss of self-respect?
■ What happens when the client experiences disapproval or rejection from others?
■ What happens when the client becomes angry?
■ How often does the client experience depression? Guilt? Sadness? Anxiety? Resentment?
■ What are the client's best assets?
■ What are five (or more) of the client's most positive qualities?

Confusion

■ What happens when the client recognizes that his/her life is out of control?
■ What happens when the client loses self-control over his/her drinking/drugging?
■ How often has the client experienced a loss of memory resulting from the abuse of drugs and/or alcohol?
■ How many times has the client been hospitalized?
■ How many times has the client been involved in traffic violations?
■ What experiences did the client have as a result of his/her first arrest and confinement?
■ What did the client feel when being arrested for the first time?
■ What did the client do after being arrested?
■ How did the client's family and friends react to the arrest and confinement?

Loss of Significant Resources

■ What is the client's state of health?
■ Does the client experience any difficulties in his/her sex life?
■ Does the client experience any difficulties in the work place resulting from drug/alcohol abuse?
■ What are these difficulties?
■ Is the client on parole? If so, how long has he/she been on parole?
■ How many real friends does the client admit to having?
■ Is the client experiencing any psychological problems?
■ What are the client's sources of income?

- How do the client's thoughts affect his/her behavior?
- Who are the most important persons in the client's life?
- What does the client believe that other people want from him/her?
- What values does the client cherish the most?

Acceptance

- Does the client really wish to stop hurting himself/herself and others?
- Does the client admit to having a problem with drugs/alcohol?
- What caused the client to seek treatment?
- What are the client's feelings about his/her use of drugs/alcohol?
- What would the client like to do more of?
- What would the client like to do less of?
- What, if any, plans does the client have for the future?
- What would happen should the client not receive assistance with his/her chemical dependency problem?
- What expectations does the client have about treatment?
- What does the client believe the treatment should do?

Resolution

- What does the client expect treatment to do for him/her?
- What amount of time does the client expect that treatment should take?
- What level of commitment is the client willing to give?
- Does the client believe that there is any hope for him/her?
- What are the client's strong points?
- What are the client's weak points?
- How will the client live without the use of drugs and/or alcohol?
- What goals, if any, has the client established?

Entry

- What are the client's greatest fears about the non-use of drugs/alcohol?
- Who, if anyone, is supportive of the client?
- What is the client's present living arrangement?
- What are the client's sources of income?
- Is the client employed? If so, provide details.
- Is the client experiencing any legal problems? If so, please explain.
- What plans has the client considered making in an effort to change his/her lifestyle?
- What problems does the client foresee?
- How will the client recognize problems, should they appear?
- What will the client do if and when such challenges appear?
- How will the client monitor himself/herself?

Establishing Rapport and Relaxation

It is important, for the initial interview to be successful, that you relax yourself and your client. During the interview, the chemically dependent client is often skeptical, apprehensive, and anxious and must overcome the fear often associated with seeing a chemical dependency counselor. In many cases, the client is unsure of those professionals who handle such problems. He or she generally doesn't know what to expect. To make matters worse, the client rarely verbalizes such concerns and questions as:

- Will she judge me?
- Will he be able to help me?
- Can I trust him?
- Can she really understand what I'm going through?
- Will she put me down?
- Will he tell me I have to use more will power?
- Will he accept me as I am?

Putting the client at ease is one of the most important challenges facing the professional counselor. It is imperative that the client understand that the counselor is sympathetic and sincerely wants to provide helpful assistance. The counselor, all the while, should show respect for the person and for any concerns that may be present.

When these attitudes are appropriately conveyed, the client will "hear" the internal signal that the situation is all right, and the counselor can begin to carefully establish rapport. Should the client's fears and hopes be ignored, reservation and frustration will most likely prevail. Upon the client's arrival, it is best to put him or her at ease by requesting basic demographic information. For instance, introduce yourself and ask for the client's name and its proper pronunciation. Ask how the client prefers to be addressed, by first or last name?

Initially, it is often wise to engage the client in "small talk." You might ask how he or she found out about you and your office or clinic. During this period, it is helpful to note whether the client settles down or becomes more tense. Some clients may want to get right to the point, whereas others will beat around the bush.

This is generally a good time to bring up the subject of confidentiality. You must assure the client that all the information you will be discussing will be kept in the strictest of confidence and that none will be shared (verbally or in written form) beyond the confines of your office or agency without written permission.

From the moment you meet your client, you should be aware of nonverbal language, for it tells you what the client is feeling. You can initiate rapport by reading these signs and by reassuring the client that he or she has done the right thing by coming in to see you.

To assist you in "reading" nonverbals, consider, for instance, how the client enters your office. How does the client move? What are the client's facial expressions?

Posture? Gait? Manner of dress? Hygiene? Skin condition? Speech? Gestures? Mood? Tone of voice? Does the client maintain eye contact? Are the eyes bloodshot? Are the pupils dilated or pinpoint? What is the condition of the fingernails?

Make note of how the client walks in—with an erect posture, chin up, full of energy? Or stooped over and moving slowly? The client may smile or may appear tense, and may avoid eye contact. The client may also exhibit tears.

Reading Signals from the Client

In addition to nonverbal signals, the client may provide clues about mental state through auditory, visual, abstract, and/or kinesthetic responses. Because the client may present problems and concerns in such subliminal ways, it is important that you pick up on voice signals (e.g., shaking or barking), vocabulary, and metaphors. Here are several examples of client responses that can provide you with valuable information.

Auditory Signals
- I hear people talking about me.
- Everything sounds loud.
- There are strange sounds in my head.

Visual Signals
- I can't see how I can ever stop using drugs/alcohol.
- The only light at the end of the tunnel is the train.
- Everything looks dark.
- I only see death for me if I continue to use drugs/alcohol.

Abstract Signals
- I can't think.
- I have no motivation.
- I feel guilty as hell for what I'm putting my family through.
- My world is gone.
- I've lost everything.
- I'm losing my mind.

Kinesthetic Signals
- It's like being among the walking dead.
- Drugs have me paralyzed.
- I feel like everything in my life is closing in around me.
- I feel the police around me.
- I feel worthless because of my alcohol abuse.

When you are able to pick up on and respond to signals like these, the client is more likely to be put at ease and feel accepted and understood.

Assessing the Level of Suffering: Compassion

Once the client has been put at ease and a certain degree of rapport has been established, you should attempt to assess the client's level of suffering. This may be accomplished by determining the facts of the particular situation and the associated emotions.

The facts of the case may include job loss, estranged family relationships, physical complaints, frequent blackouts, short-term memory loss, seizures, sexual problems, sleep difficulties, fear of going insane, decline in personal hygiene, and legal problems. The degree of emotion associated with these facts correspond to the level of suffering. Often the client is not aware of (is in denial about) why all of these things are happening.

On the other hand, the client may attempt to hide or minimize these emotions out of fear of being embarrassed or exposed as a chemically dependent person. Whatever the case, the therapist can intensify the rapport with the client in exposing the facts of the case and determining the level of suffering on the part of the client.

In determining the level of suffering, it is helpful to ask questions such as:

- What is your life like today?
- What feelings do you have about your abuse of drugs/alcohol?
- How has your use of drugs/alcohol affected your feelings about yourself?
- How would you describe your abuse of drugs/alcohol?

Encouraging clients to put their distress into words serves a dual purpose. It helps them to focus on the negatives resulting from chemical dependency, and it verifies that you are interested in their emotions and want to know about the anguish being experienced. This, in turn, strengthens the rapport you are building.

During this early phase of the initial interview, it is much more important to permit clients to "vent" their level of suffering than to categorically list all of the symptoms presenting themselves. This approach allows for a greater emphasis on the client's suffering than on your need for explicit details. Encouraging clients to bring their feelings to the forefront accomplishes several important functions:

- It permits you to assess the degree of affect and mood and to determine the underlying levels of anger, anxiety, resentment, and depression.
- It clearly demonstrates your genuine interest in what your client is feeling.
- It helps build the rapport necessary for successful treatment.

Communicating Understanding: Empathy

When your client reveals his or her suffering, it is most important that you indicate that you understand. In other words, you must show empathy. Generally speaking, empathy can be defined as communicating accurate understanding of another's feeling(s), almost as if they were one's own. This human reaction indicates care and compassion for others and helps the client to move toward health and wholeness. The primary method for demonstrating empathy is focused listening, followed by questions and responses that make it clear to the client that you understand all that he or she has confided to you.

To illustrate the use of empathy, let's imagine that you have a female client who tells you that because of her chemical dependency problem, her life has become unbearable and out of control and that she has lost all self-respect. While describing her situation, she becomes tearful and angry. She bangs on the table with her fists.

In responding to her emotional-distress signals, focus on the distress itself (as opposed to the content of her description). You may, for instance, respond with comments like this: *Sounds like your life is really out of control and you are really hurting inside. You must be tired of just being tired with the way your life is going.*

In responding in an empathetic way, you are, first, listening intently to what your client is saying and then paraphrasing (not parroting) what he or she has told you. This shows your client that you have absorbed what he or she has been telling you. It shows you understand, and understanding, of course, is critical to the success of treatment.

It is important, of course, that you be genuine and articulate in your spontaneous comments to your client's feelings. You might respond, for instance, with remarks like these:

- Your life must be awful.
- You must feel really bad about yourself.
- I can see how much you hurt and how unhappy you must be.
- I can see that your use of drugs has cost you a lot.

Although empathy is a skill that can be learned, it comes more easily to some people than to others. So if you have difficulty in showing empathy, don't try to fake it, because your client will see that you're being phony, and this certainly will have a detrimental effect on any rapport you have built thus far. Instead, ask appropriate questions to convey interest in your client's situation.

If your client appears to withdraw, check to see if you appeared genuine. For instance, ask yourself:

- Did I show by my body language that I was patient and focused on her? Or did I fidget and appear in a hurry to get the session over?

- Did I establish and maintain a level of eye contact that seemed comfortable to her?
- Did I show by my responses that I truly understand my client's situation, thoughts and feelings?

The importance of empathy in working with persons with substance-related disorders cannot be emphasized enough. It is critical that you, as a professional and caring counselor, develop an empathetic, client-centered interview style that shows genuine concern on your part.

To accomplish this, it is necessary to shift the focus away from yourself (and any anxieties and/or insecurities you yourself might have) to the thoughts, feelings, and needs of your suffering client.

Determining the Degree of Insight

In addition to communicating empathy for your client's problems, it is also necessary to understand your client's unique view of the situation. This perspective allows you to determine the degree of insight the client possesses (as opposed to the full insight you have as a measure of the reality testing that has been conducted).

When assessing and diagnosing substance-related disorders, there are three levels of insight to consider. Clients who demonstrate complete insight are able to thoroughly describe their chemical dependency symptoms. For example, a client who recognizes alcoholism as an illness that incorporates three interacting dimensions of their functioning have complete insight. Rapport generally comes very easily in this case. Such clients are able to communicate quite effectively because they recognize the symptoms of substance abuse as a part of a condition (as opposed to a part of their normal self).

The client with complete insight is generally quite open in discussing situations, thoughts, and feelings. It would be highly unlikely for this type of client to hide embarrassing details.

Partial Insight

In contrast to the client with complete insight, a person with partial insight generally lacks the awareness of even having a chemical dependency problem, usually because of some degree of denial. Since there is such a disparity in insight, you must engage the client to determine his or her ability to understand the true nature of the chemically dependent condition. A substance abuse client with partial insight generally recognizes that something is very wrong but refuses to believe that it is his or her fault. Obviously, your awareness of your client's level of insight is crucial for rapport building. The awareness allows you to phrase questions in a manner conducive to obtaining the most from the interview.

No Insight

A client who demonstrates no insight is in complete denial and, obviously, presents the most difficult challenge to you. Clients without any insight are often hostile, angry, and resistant to responding to your questions regarding their use of chemicals. It is not unusual, in fact, for these clients to be mute and passive. Some even refuse to be interviewed.

Addressing Denial

Regardless of the level of insight your client possesses, it is almost a certainty that he or she is manifesting some form of negative behavioral orientation (NBO). All addicts typically exhibit specific patterns of negative behavior regarding their use/abuse of mind-altering substances. One of the most common forms of NBO is the Declatype of Denial; it is, in fact, a central symptom of chemical dependency.

For the addict, denial generally evolves as a coping mechanism, albeit a negative one. We all use coping skills, of course, in an effort to protect ourselves, particularly during periods of high stress, and our use of such skills is generally related to our level of development. As we mature, we typically abandon faulty coping styles (like denial) and replace them with more flexible, effective, and healthy means of dealing with the stresses that come our way. This, of course, is one of your goals as a professional counselor—to help your clients abandon their ineffective coping skills (i.e., NBO). It is only then that the recovery process will take off.

As indicated throughout this text, denial is a common component of an NBO for the substance-abuse-disordered person. This Declatype can be considered on a continuum from normal to pathological. Denial can be considered normal, for example, when a young woman assures herself that her future marriage will last a lifetime. The belief may not be terribly realistic in the face of modern-day divorce statistics, but it is understandable enough—at least before reality sets in.

Denial becomes pathological when someone holds a belief that is generally not accepted by anyone else. For example, let's consider a cocaine addict who (because of addiction) has lost a hundred pounds, is sick, hospitalized, and near death. If he refuses to accept the reality of his drug-abusing behavior and assures himself and others that he will not continue his drug-taking behavior, this is definitely a case of pathological denial. And the longer the client maintains this state of unreality, the further from reality he will be.

In administering DECLARE Therapy, it is vital to understand that the development of denial is a central symptom of chemical dependency. The degree of denial is not the same for every chemically dependent person and will vary according to individual life circumstances. Whenever denial begins, however, so does the addiction.

Management of Denial

Needless to say, denial can serve a self-destructive purpose when used to continue abusive behavior. For this reason it is often one of the most difficult problems to manage in a therapeutic relationship. In fact, denial is one of the reasons many professionals avoid working with the chemically dependent (Metzger, 1988).

Nevertheless, most cases of denial should not be confronted too early in the therapy. Wallace (1986) suggests that deliberate denial, tactically used as a temporary coping device for certain life difficulties or problems, can be extremely valuable.

Denial, for instance, can be employed in adjusting to and coping with former triggers of substance abuse. This method of handling stress is, in fact, very familiar to the substance abuser. Wallace (1986) points out that in the alcoholic, increments of self-awareness and disclosure are often associated with increased anxiety, and premature reduction of denial often hinders the defenses against this anxiety—a situation that may precipitate a return to drinking.

Generally speaking, denial should be worked on gradually, and any anxiety measured that might arise from confronting it and that might trigger a return to substance abuse. When the therapist/client relationship feels secure, you can slowly raise the issue of a drug/alcohol problem. In dealing with the Declatype of Denial, timing is critical.

Declaration of Denial

The DECLARE approach allows clients to express their powerlessness over mood-altering chemicals. As emphasized throughout this text, it is extremely important for the client to *declare* this powerlessness over chemicals, because the foundation upon which recovery is built depends on the acknowledgment of this fact.

In helping your clients to acknowledge powerlessness and to break the cycle of denial, it is important that you encourage them to be honest with themselves, as well as with others. Unless a substance abuser is willing to take an honest and detailed look at the harm mood-altering chemicals have caused, there is no opportunity to clearly see the magnitude of the problem or to feel the need to change behavior patterns.

Questions for Managing Denial.   In essence, clients are urged to answer—as honestly and as openly as possible—seven questions that are based on the letters of the DECLARE acronym. A "yes" answer to any one of these questions is indicative of a drug or alcohol problem, and the respondent (or family member or friend) should seek immediate assistance from the nearest available treatment center or chemical dependency professional.

In administering these questions, it is often helpful to encourage your client to respond in writing and to give examples, even though it might be uncomfortable to do so. In *declaring* answers on paper, the client may be more likely to realize and ultimately acknowledge that a problem truly exists. Only when the client declares that there is, indeed, a problem can he or she begin to do something about it.

The DECLARE questions for managing denial in early or late chemical dependency may be used early during the interview process or at the end of either the first or second session, depending on the degree of insight the client holds. (See earlier section on Management of Denial.) Whenever possible, you should have your client respond to these questions with corroboration by a family member or friend. In DECLARE Therapy, this approach has been successful in assisting clients to decrease or eliminate their use of denial and in allowing them to take an honest look at what their use of mood-altering drugs has done to their lives. With these thoughts in mind, let's take another look at the DECLARE questions for managing denial in early or late chemical dependency.

Destructive/Dangerous Behavior

Have you ever, as a result of drinking and/or drugging, engaged in destructive and/or dangerous behavior? If so, give examples, please. (Note: Engaging in dangerous and/or destructive acts just once means there is a 50 percent chance that the client already has a problem with substance abuse.)

Eye Opener

Have you ever needed to use drugs and/or alcohol to start your day or just get through the day? If so, give examples, please. (Note: The pleasure the user feels from these "eye opener" chemicals is apparently the relief from mild withdrawal symptoms. Therefore, it appears that some degree of physical dependence is already present, indicating that use is already a severe problem.)

Control of Usage

Have you ever attempted to control or cut down your use of alcohol and/or drugs because you suspected an abuse and/or addiction problem? If so, give examples, please. (Note: The inability to control the use of mind-altering substances and/or the inability to cut down is a warning that dependency is present or impending. Even cutting down, but later slipping back up or beyond, is another sign of serious trouble.)

Loss of Resources

What resources (family, job, good health, opportunities, insurance, legal status, etc.) have you lost as a result of your alcohol and/or drug use? Give examples, please. (Note: The loss of valuable resources resulting from substance abuse is an ominous sign that a serious problem already exists.)

Anger or Annoyance

Have you ever become angry and/or annoyed when your family, friends, and/or business associates seriously discussed your drinking/ drugging habits? If so, give examples, please. (Note: Should a user become angry and/or annoyed when others suggest that his/her behavior is exceeding social limits, this is highly suggestive of a problem. Remember . . . others are generally reluctant to talk about the drinking/drugging problems of their relatives and friends.)

Remorse

Have you ever had feelings of remorse when you awoke in the morning, after being drunk or wasted the night before? If so, give examples, please. (Note: Feeling remorseful the day after suggests that there is now reason to suspect that a problem might exist.)

Esteem

How has your use of alcohol/drugs affected your feelings toward yourself and others? Give specific examples, please. (Note: This question obviously speaks to the negative feelings about one's esteem that the client has concerning the substance abuse problem. Should your client express concerns about a negative self-concept, this is a symptom of a serious problem.)

Confronting the Client

After the client has responded to the above questions in the affirmative, it is time to discuss the problem, beginning with feeding back some of the consequences that have resulted from the client's drugging/drinking behavior. Your feedback may sound something like this:

> Mr. Thomas, from what you say, you have engaged in some very dangerous behaviors while you were drinking. You have lost your job and your wife is filing for divorce. I really wonder whether the pleasures you're getting from using drugs/alcohol can be worth all the pain you're living through as a result of it.

It is important that you get the client to talk about the problem by administering the questions. Don't allow him or her to generalize, but instead, have your client zero in on the examples provided by the questions. For instance:

- How do you feel about having to go to prison for a crime you committed while under the influence?

- How do you feel about yourself after getting high and going to bed with a stranger?
- How do you feel about your wife finding out about this behavior?
- How do you feel about the people you injured or killed in that auto accident while you were drunk?
- How do you feel about the lies you told your family because of your use of drugs/alcohol?

Whatever approach you take with your questions, the important thing here is to confront, confront, confront! Your confrontation may be soft—that is, using a quiet voice to present messages that combine caring with confrontation. Or it may be hard—employing a harsh, tough, and confrontational tone, appropriate to the set of circumstances you have uncovered.

Generally speaking, hard confrontation is held as a last resort, as it tends to arouse anxiety in clients who are quite indifferent to anything but this type of tactic. Should such a client display anxiety, however, it is appropriate to promote this sort of discomfort. In fact, a paradoxical technique here is to first arouse anxiety through hard confrontation, and then get the client to discuss whether he or she is satisfied with the effects alcohol/drugs have produced on day-to-day living. As the client begins to show concern about these matters, slowly withdraw your involvement (Metzger, 1988). Stay with this approach, confronting the client until denial lessens.

As you guide your client toward taking action about his or her using, it is appropriate to act as a positive role model. In fact, in DECLARE Therapy, the clinician (ideally) is a source of hope, strength, and appropriate judgment to the client. For example, you may say:

> It's abundantly clear to me that your drinking and drugging is creating problems in your life. Since you agree with me, I'm hopeful that you also agree the only way to stop the problem is to stop using. Will you do that?

Case Studies

To further show how the DECLARE line of questioning works in a clinical setting, following are excerpts from two case studies (recorded with the permission of the clients, whose names have been changed). These interview segments demonstrate how the DECLARE questions were used to assist these clients in zeroing in on their use of drugs and alcohol and on the negative consequences that resulted.

Case Study No. 1

The first segment is taken from an interview with Mr. Sanders, a 36-year-old white male alcoholic, recently released from prison and being treated in a drug and alcohol treatment facility.

DR. TAYLOR: Mr. Sanders, do you consider yourself an addict or alcoholic?

MR. SANDERS: Not really sure at this time. Others have said I am.

DR. TAYLOR: I have a series of questions that I wish to ask you regarding your use of drugs and alcohol. I would like for you to answer "yes" or "no" to each question. However, if your reply is "yes," I would like for you to provide me with as many examples as you can to illustrate your answer. Your answers may help us to determine whether or not you are chemically dependent.

MR. SANDERS: All right.

DR. TAYLOR: Have you ever, as a result of drinking and/or drugging, engaged in any destructive and/or dangerous behavior? If so, give examples, please.

MR. SANDERS: (Pause) Yes . . . as far as my driving an automobile . . . at a lot faster speed than what I normally would . . . as a result of being drunk. I was also involved in several domestic violence charges. All that is because of my drinking. It was my fault; but I was drinking at the time. I get violent . . . when someone more or less provokes me or I put myself in the position for it to happen.

DR. TAYLOR: Have you ever needed to use drugs and/or alcohol to start your day or just get through the day? If so, give examples, please.

MR. SANDERS: Yes, many times. Lots of times after waking up with a hangover, feeling bad from drinking the night before. I'll start drinking again and for a long time that was the main reason that I drank—to get through the day. I didn't think I could function or that I could deal with my problems and stress and pressure without drinking . . . so I used it as a crutch or some false courage.

DR. TAYLOR: Have you attempted to control or cut down on your use of alcohol and/or drugs? If so, give examples, please.

MR. SANDERS: Yes, I thought if I maybe tried to just switch to beer, it wouldn't be so bad . . . then I thought maybe I'll drink just on the weekend . . . it always started from that first drink . . . just an ongoing thing.

DR. TAYLOR: What resources (health, family, job, insurance, opportunities) have you lost as a result of your alcohol/drug use?

MR. SANDERS: As far as my health . . . I've been pretty fortunate that I don't have any serious medical problems from my drinking. As far as my family . . . my family really don't know me that well . . . other than my drinking. They don't know me when I'm sober . . . all they know is my drinking. As far as a job . . . I've been fired a few times on jobs. I've quit a lot of times because I know I was on the verge of getting fired because of my drinking. I lost my best friend . . . and what little material things that I had, I lost all of them behind my drinking.

DR. TAYLOR: Is there anything else you can think of? Did you ever lose your freedom?

MR. SANDERS: Yes. That's one thing I didn't think of, but that, too. I lost a lot of mental progress that I feel I could have had without the drinking. How far it put me back, I'm not sure. At 36 years old and just starting out . . . I could have been further advanced, I'm sure, without the alcohol.

DR. TAYLOR: Are you saying that you could have accomplished more with your life had you not been so consumed with drinking?

MR. SANDERS: Yes. I really feel I could have. I feel I could have; and still, I can do quite a bit at this age.

DR. TAYLOR: Have you ever gotten angry or annoyed with family, friends, or business associates who seriously discussed your drinking and drugging? If so, give examples, please.

MR. SANDERS: Yes. More or less. I felt a little angry, a little frustrated; annoyed, because at the time, in the back of my head I knew they were telling the truth. They would tell me things like, "You know you need to try and slow down . . . you need to try to leave that stuff alone." But when I get to drinking, everything just goes. I would get annoyed because I didn't want to hear that; because in the back of my head, I knew they were telling the truth.

DR. TAYLOR: Have you ever had feelings of remorse when you awoke in the morning after having been drunk or wasted the night before? If so, give examples, please.

MR. SANDERS: Remorse is the same thing as guilt or feelings of being sorry?

DR. TAYLOR: Yes.

MR. SANDERS: Yes. Lots of times. For instance, after I've been drinking . . . I get mad at somebody or something, for whatever reason. I might have to break their window . . . and then the next day, I was really sorry about it. You know, you go and apologize and all that . . . pay for the window and stuff; and you still feel bad about it; but, turn around a couple of weeks or so later and do something else . . . it's just a fact . . . I've done it so many times.

DR. TAYLOR: Can you think of any other times when you felt this way after getting drunk or wasted?

MR. SANDERS: Once when I woke up in jail for public intoxication, I would look back and say, "Here I am again doing this." I don't know why I keep on doing this . . . but, yet, I still do . . . I just keep on doing it. Then sometimes I get to looking at all the things I could have had . . . or what I was on the verge of getting; and lost because of my drinking. Get paid a nice little piece of money . . . and wake up the next day, broke.

DR. TAYLOR: How has your use of drugs or alcohol affected your feelings toward yourself and others? Give examples, please.

MR. SANDERS: Bad feelings about myself!

DR. TAYLOR: Have your feelings of self-esteem been affected? How?

MR. SANDERS: Yes! Yes! For a long time while I was drinking . . . my self-esteem was pretty low. No self-esteem, no confidence in myself for nothing. It was pretty low.

DR. TAYLOR: All right. That's all of the questions. You've answered "yes" to each of the questions I posed to you. Now do you believe there's a problem . . . that you're an alcoholic?

MR. SANDERS: You know, Doc. After answering these questions, I really do have a problem. I guess I am an alcoholic. What do you think?

DR. TAYLOR: I think you do have a serious problem and that we need to discuss it in more detail. What do you think of the questions you just answered?

MR. SANDERS: I kind of like them because they give me time (pause) . . . to exercise my mind . . . get my mind stimulated about drinking . . . my true thoughts and what not. I do have a problem.

In Mr. Sanders' case, the questions allowed him to bring greater focus to his drinking and to the problems it has caused in his life. Through this approach, he was able to take an honest look at himself and to begin the process of loosening his grip on denial.

Case Study No. 2

The second case concerns Mr. Lewis, a 25-year-old white male. Mr. Lewis is currently in his first year of sobriety since his incarceration five years ago for aggravated robbery, for which he was sentenced to five to twenty-five years. Prior to his arrest, Mr. Lewis states, he was at the height of his addiction, using thirty to forty grams of cocaine weekly. He also reports consuming about two-and-one-half fifths of alcohol daily. Alcohol, he says, is his drug of choice.

Mr. Lewis also reports that he used both cocaine and alcohol during his first four years of incarceration. During the past year, however, he says that his drug and alcohol use has stopped. The explanation he provides for this decision is that there may be a relationship between his past use and present incarceration.

Once again, the DECLARE questions were used to assist the client in focusing on his use of drugs and alcohol and in *declaring* their negative impact on his life. Mr. Lewis has recently been released from prison and is now on parole. He is currently receiving treatment for his addiction in an inpatient drug and alcohol treatment facility. The following are excerpts from his initial interview:

DR. TAYLOR: Mr. Lewis, I'd like to ask you a number of questions, and after each, please respond with either "yes" or "no." If your reply is "yes," please give me examples to illustrate your point.

MR. LEWIS: All right.

DR. TAYLOR: Have you ever, as a result of drinking and/or drugging, engaged in destructive or dangerous behavior?

MR. LEWIS: Yeah. I drive cars fast (*smiles*) . . . and I used to like to . . . like to climb buildings. We have a game we called "widget" and the more dangerous it became, the better we liked it. We would get to doing acid and drinking . . . you know those construction sites with the scaffolding on the side of the building? That's where we played "widget."

DR. TAYLOR: Any other examples?

MR. LEWIS: Not really.

DR. TAYLOR: Did you get into fights?

MR. LEWIS: I was all the time fighting . . . constant fighting. See, I was in a gang; and there was another gang . . . Now the other gang . . . did not come over where we were; and we didn't go where they were. But there was this big park; and we would meet at the house in the park . . . and fight.

DR. TAYLOR: Have you ever needed to use drugs or alcohol in order to start your day or just to get through a day?

MR. LEWIS: I needed drugs. I needed alcohol to get up and out of bed. I needed alcohol for lunch; and sometimes I would get so depressed . . . I would go to the state store and get me something to drink; or better, I'd go down to the bar and I'd sit there in the bar. Then I'd go at it . . . it would be daylight . . . but when I came out, it would be dark and I'd go home and to bed.

DR. TAYLOR: Have you attempted to control or cut down your alcohol or drug use?

MR. LEWIS: Well . . . I started hanging out with people who didn't drink. OK, then I started getting involved in church activities. Went around church people I knew wouldn't drink.

DR. TAYLOR: Was that an effort to at least control your drinking by being around people who didn't use, like your other friends?

MR. LEWIS: Yes, it was.

DR. TAYLOR: Did it work?

MR. LEWIS: Yeah . . . for a while.

DR. TAYLOR: How long?

MR. LEWIS: Not long . . . I found out it didn't work.

DR. TAYLOR: What resources (health, family, job, friends, opportunities) have you lost resulting from your alcohol or drug use?

MR. LEWIS: I lost my job . . . my family. I just lost everything I had. I lost it. I lost control of myself. Whatever you think alcohol can do, it can do more . . . it can take everything you got and more. I lost everything I had, including my self-respect. I lost that. I just lost everything I had . . . especially my family . . . that hurts me most . . . and my son who is 10 years old.

DR. TAYLOR: Have you ever had feelings of remorse when you woke up in the morning after being drunk or wasted the night before?

MR. LEWIS: When you say remorse, what do you mean?

DR. TAYLOR: Have you ever had any real bad feelings about some of the things you've done or said?

MR. LEWIS: Yeah . . . I used to have this girlfriend; she was real cute . . . real pretty. I would get drunk and would get mad because she wouldn't have sex with me . . . she never had sex before. Anyway, when I would sober up and she would tell me things I said to her and the things I done to her . . . well, we finally broke up. She said when I got drunk, I was like a Dr. Jekyll and Mr. Hyde. She said, "I just can't deal with you when you're drinking. I'm scared you're gonna hurt me." I felt remorse.

I wonder what I done the night before. I used to have quite a few blackouts . . . people would tell me, "Man, you know what you did last night?" I would say, "No. What'd I do?" They would tell me and I would tell them they were all damn lies. I didn't do anything like that . . . then I got to thinking maybe I am doing crazy things. I used to call it drinking myself into stupidness.

DR. TAYLOR: What do you mean by that?

MR. LEWIS: Drinking and having blackouts . . . you do things and you don't remember doing them. When you black out, you don't remember it . . . I would drink myself into ignorance, stupidness. You know, I used to drink two-and-a-half fifths alone in a day.

DR. TAYLOR: That much?

MR. LEWIS: I know this old man who worked construction for twenty years. This guy drank a fifth of alcohol a day for twenty years. This guy would work five or six floors in the air and had his bottle with him; and at lunch time, go to the store and get another, and leave it alone until the next day and he would start all over again the next day. You know, sometimes I think I tried to be just like him. I don't know . . . it's just a reason for drinking. It's stupid, anyway. You can come up with a million reasons why you should drink; but try to come up with one why you shouldn't.

DR. TAYLOR: Interesting.

MR. LEWIS: You can't do it. If you want to know something . . . go ask a drunk. A drunk knows. A drunk's got the answer to everything. Ask a drunk and he'll tell you. He may be full of shit; but he has the answers.

DR. TAYLOR: How has your use of drugs and alcohol affected your feelings about yourself?

MR. LEWIS: I'm telling you . . . sometimes I would want to die. I often felt sorry for myself . . . I don't know why. Sometimes I would wake up with a hangover and would think, "I got to quit this. I got to quit this. I'm killing myself and my family. I've got to quit."

Yeah. It affected my feelings about myself to where, maybe, I was going off into self-pity . . . but I would not stop drinking. As a matter of fact, I would drink more.

DR. TAYLOR: Can you explain how your negative feelings toward yourself made you drink more?

MR. LEWIS: I don't know. Sometimes when I was drinking, I felt like nothing. That whenever I had a few beers, I would go down to the bar with the rest of the drunks. I felt needed. I felt like I was part of something, instead of being a castaway from everything. I was part of something. I ain't quite figured out what it is, but I was part of it, whatever it was. Then when I was sober, I felt sorry for myself . . . going into that pity thing.

I wish I could quit this . . . why do I drink so much? Especially when I go out and spend three or four hundred dollars. Later go back home and not have ten dollars in my pocket. Ain't no bills got paid . . . I would say, "I got to quit this. I can't do this anymore." Feeling sorry for myself and wanted to quit drinking, but never would. Oh, hell. I would say I can quit anything I want; but I never would stop. I made a lot of enemies out there during my drinking. At least the people I called my friends, they sort of turned against me because I was so wild. They would tell me that I would say things toward them that would hurt their feelings.

DR. TAYLOR: Mr. Lewis, are you an alcoholic?

MR. LEWIS: Yes! There is no doubt in my mind. Believe it or not, this is only the second time in my life that I have ever admitted that to anyone (looks away). I am an alcoholic. It's hard to say the words.

In Mr. Lewis's case, the use of the DECLARE questions helped him to focus more clearly on his abuse of alcohol and to finally make the connection between use and incarceration. It was a painful revelation both to discover and to admit to another person that he was really an alcoholic. However, by making this *declaration* of chemical dependency, he was able to see the need to change his behavior.

Inpatient or Outpatient Services?

Early during the initial interview, the clinician must make a determination about whether or not the client requires inpatient or outpatient services. To determine if the client requires inpatient services, the following information should be gathered:

■ **Establish the severity of withdrawal symptoms to be expected.** For example, is the client displaying symptoms of withdrawal that might be life-threatening? Does the client require supervised detoxification in order to prevent further use? Are the client's current levels of use adversely interfering with his or her ability to prevent further use? It is also important to determine how many (if any) detoxification attempts have failed in the past. Finally, do current abuse levels represent a chronic inability to avoid use?

■ **Determine any chronic medical conditions.** This is important in cases where there is some related illness that could prove dangerous and require medical intervention. Does the client, for instance, have a history that would require medical monitoring—for example, hypertension, liver dysfunction, gastrointestinal disorders, and so forth? If the client is female, is she pregnant?

■ **Assess the client's mental status.** Is the client, for example, oriented in all three spheres—time, place, and person? Assess whether or not past attempts at abstinence have produced disruptions in the client's orientation. Also determine the type(s) of medication the client is presently taking and if he or she is on psychotropic drugs. Establish if the client is displaying signs or symptoms of a mental illness or has a history of such disease. Finally, assess if the client has any homicidal or suicidal tendencies.

■ **Assess the client's attempts at abstinence.** This is important in determining whether or not the client can refrain from use for seventy-two hours (three days) without supervision. Also, determine if the client is currently abstinent and how much subjective distress he or she is experiencing. Does there appear to be any danger of imminent relapse? Ask if the client is residing with others who are themselves using and who are not supportive of abstinence. Does the client have any barriers that would prevent involvement in outpatient services?

If these symptoms are absent, the client is suitable for outpatient services.

Assessment: Two Scales

Assessment is a vital component of the ongoing process of evaluation of those identified as having substance-related disorders. Only through comprehensive assessment can the needs of the chemically dependent be accurately determined. With appropriate information, the clinician can make important decisions in assisting the clients in regaining control over their lives.

THQ-R Assessment

As discussed in Chapter 2, the Taylor Historical Questionnaire-Revised (THQ-R), which is divided into two parts, is a comprehensive instrument that assesses drug-related, alcohol-related, and psychiatric symptoms. The first part of the scale gathers general biographical information, biological data, drug use history, drug treatment history, alcohol use and treatment history, and legal history. The second part pertains to the seven DECLARE modalities.

The THQ-R should be administered during the initial interview. Should the client demonstrate an inability to read or refuses for some reason to complete the form, the clinician should use the THQ-R as part of a structured interview for gathering needed information about the client.

The THQ-R is designed to determine the extent of substance abuse and its physical, psychological, familial, social, and legal consequences. With this instrument, the pattern(s) of use of all types of abusable substances is(are) assessed, with the following factors considered:

1. Dosage
2. Quality
3. Duration of use/abuse
4. Expenses incurred with the procurement of substances
5. Method(s) used to administer the substances
6. Family issues
7. Interpersonal relationships
8. Existence or nonexistence of enablers
9. Physical effects
10. Emotional effects

11. Psychological effects
12. Tolerance levels
13. Withdrawal
14. Overdoses
15. Specific psychopathology (which should be well documented prior to treatment)
16. Legal status
17. Treatment history

DAPIR-R Assessment

As we also saw in Chapter 2, another valuable assessment procedure, and one that is simple to administer, is the Draw-A-Person-In-The-Rain Anxiety Scale–Revised (DAPIR-R), which assesses the level of anxiety experienced by the addict or alcoholic. The anxiety level is represented by the rain. For the convenience of the reader, we repeat here the description of the scale given earlier.

The subject is given a sheet of 8½- by 11-inch, unlined, white bond paper and a sharpened no. 2 pencil with eraser and is asked to "Draw a person in the rain."

The scoring manual, designed to assess anxiety, includes indices that may be scored as 1, 2, 3, 4, or 5. In addition, a table of norms and T-score values, percentiles, means and standard deviations, reliabilities, and a psychogram are provided so that the clinician can determine the level of anxiety of the client.

Recapping . . .

■ Although the goals of the DECLARE clinician are similar to those of other professional therapists, points of departure exist in the conduct of the initial interview.

■ In essence, the therapist focuses on seven modalities: Denial, Esteem, Confusion, Loss of Significant Resources, Acceptance, Resolution, and Entry.

■ Central to the success of the method is the ability of the clinician to put the client at ease and to establish an empathetic, client-centered, caring interview style.

■ By using empathy to focus on the client, the clinician is better able to determine his or her level of suffering.

■ After communicating empathy, it is important to determine the client's level of insight (if any) into the alcohol/drug abuse problem.

■ Before successful treatment can be expected, it is important that the client *declare* his or her powerlessness over the abusing behavior. In other words, Denial must be managed.

■ The questions for managing denial also produce the DECLARE acronym: Destructive/Dangerous Behavior, Eye Opener, Control of Usage, Loss of Resources, Anger or Annoyance, Remorse, and Esteem.

■ Once the client has responded to these questions, the clinician must attempt confrontation, carefully encouraging and guiding the client toward taking action against the problem.

■ During the initial interview, the clinician determines whether or not inpatient or outpatient treatment is appropriate.

■ Assessment is a vital component of the ongoing process of evaluating persons identified as having substance-related disorders. DECLARE Therapy encourages the use of two assessment scales: the THQ-R and the DAPIR-R.

■ This chapter details several important procedures to be used during the initial interview, but clinicians interested in this approach should keep in mind that individual circumstances and needs will determine the specific format of the initial and subsequent interview(s). Nevertheless, the sequence of events presented in this chapter is fairly typical and should be followed as closely as possible.

CHAPTER

4 Diagnosis and Treatment

In DECLARE Therapy the therapist's diagnostic impressions and ratings define the need for treatment, which is based on reports of the amount, duration, and intensity of signs and symptoms within each specific modality considered. The therapist should keep in mind that diagnostic impressions and ratings are not merely intended as estimates of the client's potential benefit from treatment. They also are used to determine the extent to which treatment is required.

This chapter briefly reviews the contents of the first two chapters, further developing the concept of the Modality Profile. It then discusses therapeutic procedures relating to diagnosis and treatment and to pre- and post-treatment concerns within the context of the DECLARE model of therapy. It concludes with an illustration of the practical application of these diagnostic and treatment procedures, presented through two extensive case studies.

Preliminary Evaluation: A Review

Assessing the Client

Following is a brief summary of the primary components of the DECLARE assessment procedure.

- Administer the THQ-R and DAPIR-R.
- Define the client's presenting problem(s).
- Determine the client's behavior orientation (NBO or PBO).
- Discuss how the problem of drug/alcohol use has disrupted the functioning of the client, including both severity and duration.
- Establish the antecedent events and consequences.
- Specify the maintaining problem(s).
- Decide what the client must change and how this change will be effected.
- Make a list of the client's strengths and weaknesses.
- Discuss any other treatment the client has undergone.

- Conduct a mental status examination, a violence assessment, and a suicide assessment.
- Conduct a drug and alcohol screen.

Making Contact

During the initial interview the clinician should be aware that the client may be skeptical of the clinician-client relationship. Here are some practical suggestions for dealing with this situation as well as with others that typically present themselves during the course of treatment.

- Be professional.
- Attempt to establish a comfortable rapport.
- Avoid imposing personal judgment.
- Reassure the client that the therapist-client relationship is confidential.
- Determine the motivation for drug/alcohol use, as well as the effects and treatment.
- Explain the importance of regular drug and alcohol screening tests.
- Be aware of the "con." (When the client exhibits this sort of behavior, confront it directly. Whenever possible, obtain collateral information.)
- Always give your client feedback on your observations during this initial assessment session.
- Try to enlist your client's assistance in the treatment process.
- Reinforce the notion of complete abstinence.
- Emphasize to the client the need to give up drug-abusing friends and relatives.

It is important that both the therapist and the client *declare* goals and objectives. In doing so, it is helpful to keep the following suggestions in mind:

- Specify for the client a time frame for what will be done.
- Discuss how you plan to handle the client in terms of working with him/her and in terms of your projected procedures and goals.
- Explain what the client should and should not expect from the treatment.

Note that upon completion of a specific period of time in treatment, the client is assessed regarding the recovery process. This is accomplished by using criteria set forth in the Biphasic Analysis Reintegration Sequence (BARS) instrument, which monitors the entry/reentry phase of recovery (see Chapter 5). Further note that in order to maintain continuity of care, it is suggested that the clinician use progress notes with each contact made with the client. Keep a fact sheet handy during sessions to record data pertinent to the case study, such as the client's current problems; the initial dates of the occurrence of the problems, the agents deemed responsible, and the dates of resolution or disposition.

Developing the Modality Profile

Before developing a Modality Profile the clinician must be assured (by the results of drug screening tests) that the client is completely withdrawn from drugs and alcohol. Additionally, the clinician should observe for signs that the client is free from any indications of psychosis and suicidal or homicidal ideations. With these determinations in place, the following steps should be followed in developing a Modality Profile (see also Chapter 2).

1. During the initial interview session, administer the THQ-R.
2. During the second session, discuss the THQ-R and ask specific questions concerning items that are unclear or ambiguous.
3. Before the third session, peruse information gathered from spouse and/or other persons significant to the client, and draw up the initial Modality Profile. You may want to request that your client also create a Modality Profile.
4. Review the initial Modality Profile to determine who and/or what is maintaining the problem.
5. Determine what modalities stand out among the rest.
6. Study the Modality Profile.
7. Share with the client your impressions, observations, and assumptions—using clinical judgment, of course, in the amount of information you provide.
8. Upon completion of the Modality Profile, discuss with your client each item within each modality. This will help eliminate any ambiguities. To appreciate the functional significance of the problem(s), discuss each in terms of antecedents and consequences.
9. Ask the client if there is any pertinent information that was not included in the THQ-R.
10. Establish mutually agreed-upon immediate and long-term goals.
11. Decide on the treatment approaches and resources to be utilized—e.g., self-management, problem solving, cognitive and behavioral-skills training, social skills, job skills, leisure and lifestyle planning, and relapse prevention.
12. Use the MAC-D-R to record all relevant information gathered from all sources during the assessment phase. (See later discussion on Using the MAC-D-R.)

To appreciate the advantages of developing a Modality Profile rather than using more conventional drug and alcohol abuse assessment procedures see The Case of M.K. at the end of the chapter.

Diagnosis: Using the DSM-IV-TR

In the field of substance-related disorders, the *Diagnostic and Statistical Manual of Mental Disorders, 4th edition* (DSM-IV-TR) (American Psychiatric Association,

2000) is a useful guide. The manual offers two basic classifications: (1) substance-induced organic psychotic disorders and (2) substance-related disorders. In the first category, the criteria are principally substance-specific intoxication or the withdrawal state. Thus, if a client appears high and declares he used PCP, the probable diagnosis would be "Phencyclidine Intoxication" (292.89). A "substance-related disorders" diagnosis applies when the individual:

- Meets the substance-specific criteria
- Is not obviously in a condition of intoxication
- Is not showing signs of withdrawal

The clinician should keep in mind that some individuals with a substance-related disorder may have had, at some juncture, a substance-induced psychotic disorder.

For all classes of substance-related disorders, pathological use is categorized as either Substance Dependence or the residual diagnosis of Substance Abuse. These diagnoses also allow for further course specifiers of the disorder, for example, with Physiological Dependence Withdrawal, Physiological Dependence, Early Full Remission, Early Partial Remission, Sustained Full Remission, Sustained Partial Remission on Agonist Therapy and in a controlled environment. Also, the maladaptive pattern used in Substance Abuse is indicated by either continued or recurrent use of the substance. The diagnosis is made only if symptoms occur within a twelve-month period.

Because drug abusers are likely to be polydrug users and abusers, it is technically correct to give them multiple diagnoses on AXIS I for the various drugs they use. By convention, however, when diagnosing we generally place on AXIS I only those drugs which require treatment or those that become the focus of concern. On AXIS II the clinician records both personality and developmental disorders. AXIS III permits the clinician to report any current condition or physical disorder, the knowledge of which would be helpful in the treatment and management of the client. AXIS IV is for reporting psychosocial and environmental problems that may affect the diagnosis, treatment, and prognosis of mental disorders. AXIS V allows the clinician to evaluate the client's overall level of psychological, social, and occupational functioning on the Global Assessment of Functioning (GAF) scale.

Clinicians should obtain a copy of the DSM-IV and become familiar with the diagnostic process. Although they may not always agree with the diagnostic criteria set forth in the manual, they must be thoroughly familiar with the diagnostic categories.

Treatment Plan

After the diagnosis has been reached, the clinician and the client should agree on a treatment plan. It is good policy to explore the proposed course of treatment with the client to determine any resistance that may be present and to attempt to reach mutually agreed-upon goals and objectives. The clinician should assess any treatment history to determine whether any previous attempts at abstinence have been tried. This information is important because it provides a good clue about ego strength, and it alerts the clinician to any adverse or refractory behaviors.

As repeatedly emphasized, DECLARE Therapy recognizes the need for a multifaceted approach to the treatment of substance-related disorders. Although the approach focuses on the individual and the family, it can also be used effectively with groups, with the intent of providing emotional support to facilitate change for each member of the group. In either case, as you may recall from Chapter 1, the therapeutic approach is biopsychosocial in nature, involving the interaction of biological (genetic), psychological (host), and social (environmental) aspects of the individual's life.

Included in the biological factors are genetic materials and processes through which the person inherits characteristics from his or her parents, that is, acquired Declatypes (see Chapter 1). These inherited characteristics include aspects of the individual's physiological functioning. For example, structural brain damage that causes impaired cognitive functioning may also impair the functioning of the immune system and thus prevent it from protecting the body from external antigens.

Psychosocial factors include the behavioral and mental processes of:

- Cognitions
- Emotions
- Motivation

Cognitions, in effect, are mental activities that encompass abilities such as perceiving, learning, remembering, believing, and problem solving. Emotions, on the other hand, are subjective feelings arising from our behavior, thoughts, and physiology. Many of our emotions, of course, are positive and some are negative.

An individual whose emotions are negative may be more likely to engage in drug-abusing behaviors than one whose emotions are more positive. In exploring the motivation behind the abusive behavior, the therapist asks two basic questions:

- Why does the client behave that way?
- Why did this person choose to use drugs rather than some other, more acceptable, form of behavior?

Many persons are motivated to do what their peers do. They reason, "If my best friend uses, then I should, too." Of course, we all live in a social world in which interpersonal relationships are important. Whenever we interact with others, we affect them and they, in turn, affect us. This is a small but integral aspect of the social system.

Many levels or layers in society make up the community, culture, society, nations, and, finally the world at large. We—the chemically dependent and non-chemically-dependent alike—are, therefore, affected by more than just our friends. As we all know only too well, the mass media, in the form of advertisements, TV commercials, and movies, often encourage us in overt as well as subliminal messages to smoke cigarettes, to use both legal and illegal drugs, and to drink alcoholic beverages excessively.

In following the biopsychosocial approach, the clinician seeks to provide whatever the client requires, drawing upon the resources inside as well as outside the therapeutic model—including his or her own professionally informed wellsprings of intuition and creativity. In tailoring the DECLARE model to a client's specific profile, the clinician will consider the need for group counseling; education and health programs; legal advice; employment assistance; social services; family counseling; recreational opportunities; pregnancy counseling; nutritional counseling; self-help groups (Alcoholics Anonymous, Cocaine Anonymous, Narcotics Anonymous), training and ancillary services, and so forth. In summary, the clinician must constantly be aware of the needs of the client and provide for those needs in the best and most efficient manner possible.

Degree of Treatment

In rating a client's need for treatment, a structural profile (in the form of a bar graph) can serve as a helpful, immediate reminder of both the therapist's and the client's evaluations. The chart should include the following indicators:

1. Treatment not indicated (no problem)
2. Treatment probably not necessary (slight difficulty)
3. Some treatment necessary (moderate problem)
4. Treatment necessary (considerable difficulty)
5. Treatment absolutely required (extreme difficulty)

In talking with a client, it is important for the therapist to determine the validity of the client's statements. If behavioral signals, for example, clearly suggest that the client is not being truthful or is making conflicting, unjustifiable statements, then the therapist must make judgments about the validity of the information. The therapist confidence rating uses the following evaluative categories:

a. Client distorts information: 1 = *no*; 2 = *yes*
b. Client's level of impairment causes an inability to understand what is being asked: 1 = *no*; 2 = *yes*

Prognosis

Using a seven-point scale based on the seven therapeutic modalities, with definitions assigned to each point, the prognostic rating system of DECLARE Therapy provides a detailed, objective view of the client's level of functioning or dysfunctioning. Following the acronym, the prognostic criteria are as follows:

Prognosis Criteria

D. Denial of the chemical dependency process

E. External motivation

C. Change of environment

L. Life skills for sobriety

A. Awareness of chemical dependency process

R. Recent history of sobriety

E. Evidence of willingness and commitment to change lifestyle

Defined according to four levels of behavioral expression, or development, these criteria serve to produce the Clinical Prognosis Guidelines of DECLARE Therapy. In effect, the seven-point scale produces four levels of prognosis, as follows:

1. Poor Prognosis:
   D. Denies chemical dependency process
   E. Lacks internal motivation to stop using/abusing
   C. Unwilling to change environment
   L. Lacks life skills necessary for sobriety
   A. Lacks awareness of chemical dependency process
   R. Lacks a history of sobriety
   E. Lacks willingness to change lifestyles
2. Guarded Prognosis:
   D. Annoyed with others regarding chemical dependency process
   E. Some internal motivation to stop drinking/ drugging
   C. Some willingness to change environment
   L. Has some life skills for sobriety
   A. Has some education for sobriety
   R. Has some period of sobriety
   E. Has some willingness to change lifestyle
3. Fair Prognosis:
   D. Willing to seriously look at using/abusing
   E. Moderately internally motivated to stop using
   C. Moderately willing to change environment
   L. Exhibits some life skills for sobriety
   A. Has increased knowledge of chemical dependency
   R. Exhibits increasing periods of sobriety
   E. Clearly exhibits willingness to change lifestyle
4. Good Prognosis:
   D. Breakdown of denial—i.e., "I DECLARE I am chemically dependent."
   E. Internal motivation to stop using
   C. Willingness to change environment
   L. Appropriate life skills for sobriety
   A. Definite knowledge of the chemical dependency process
   R. Recent history of sobriety
   E. Commitment to make required lifestyle changes

Ongoing Assessment

Because the assessment process is an ongoing one, any changes observed serve as important benchmarks in developing and adjusting the treatment plan. Such assessment provides the clinician with concrete, consistent means for evaluating client progress or lack of progress. A professional who reviews a client's record should be able easily to understand:

- Client's problems
- What other professionals are thinking about each of the problem areas
- Logic and necessity of the diagnostic plan implemented
- Rationalization of the treatment plan
- Results to date

The therapist should also recognize that the criteria for establishing the rating of any problem may vary from situation to situation. Thus, the scales described above were developed to provide, as much as possible, a standardized score.

Client Rating.   The client should be given the opportunity to rate himself or herself on each modality, expressing the extent to which he or she feels treatment is necessary. At the conclusion of the assessment of each modality, the client should be directed to give one of the following ratings concerning the need for treatment:

1. None   2. Mild   3. Moderate
4. Severe   5. Extreme   6. Catastrophic

This rating becomes a part of the treatment record.

Using the MAC-D-R.   The Multifaceted Assessment of Chemical Dependency Inventory–Revised (MAC-D-R) form should be used to record problems and issues within each modality and to assess the effectiveness of treatment. Each set of progress notes should logically follow the progress of the client's problem and stand on its own in clearly explicating change or the lack of change. The clinician should be sure to date the progress notes and indicate the number and nature of the problem discussed, using the form provided in the Modality Profile–oriented format. Clients, of course, may present themselves in any one of the seven modalities. For convenience, therefore, the therapist is encouraged to use the letters of the acronym to identify the pertinent modalities.

Following is an extensive listing, within each of the DECLARE modalities, of the problems or issues the clinician may address during the initial and subsequent interviews. The clinician, however, should not assume that these are the only areas of concern. In fact, the clinician is encouraged to generate additional information that he or she feels is necessary to gain a better understanding of the problems and issues confronting the client. Keep in mind that information gained at this time is used in conjunction with that obtained by the Taylor Historical Questionnaire–Revised.

- **Modality I—Denial.** In determining the client's level of denial concerning substance abuse problems, the therapist should observe and investigate the following:
  1. Client's feelings/mood
  2. Client's avoidance/indifference/evasiveness
  3. Drug activities
  4. Progress of drug problem(s)
  5. Client's plans
  6. Client's concerns and problems
  7. Blaming others
  8. Level of resistance
  9. Client's level of involvement (passivity)
  10. Client's evaluation of the need for treatment
  11. Therapist ratings indicating a need for treatment in this modality
  12. Client's motivation, internal vs. external
  13. Therapist's ratings indicating a need for treatment in this modality

- **Modality II—Esteem.** In evaluating the client's sense of self-esteem, the therapist should observe such aspects as appearance, mood, thoughts, activities, and behavior and consider the following:
  1. Loss of self-respect
  2. Disapproval/rejection
  3. Impairment of motivation
  4. Depression/guilt/sadness/shame
  5. Anger
  6. Negative self-image
  7. Client's evaluation of the need for treatment
  8. Client's motivational level
  9. Therapist's ratings indicating a need for treatment in this modality

- **Modality III—Confusion.** In evaluating confusion, the clinician will focus on what the client reveals regarding experience of and reactions to a chaotic and disorganized lifestyle and to feelings of being controlled by demands of the drug(s) being abused. Areas to be considered include the following:
  1. Results of a mental status examination (may be administered prior to the evaluation of this modality)
  2. Loss of control over the effects of the drug(s)
  3. Memory loss/distortion (long and short term)
  4. Suspicion of others
  5. Traffic violation(s)
  6. Negative attitude(s)
  7. Arrests/confinements

8. Client's motivational level
9. Client's evaluation of the need for treatment
10. Therapist's ratings indicating a need for treatment for this modality

■ **Modality IV—Loss of Significant Resources.** Next, the clinician asks the client to report the loss of important possessions—good health, family, friends, employment, finances, legal status, and so forth. The analysis of this modality should include information in the following areas:

1. Results of a physical examination
2. Results of a psychological examination
3. Employment problems (Verify any job loss with a reliable source, including name, address, and phone number.)
4. Marital discord (spouse abuse, child abuse)
5. Current legal status (controlled environment: jail, prison, drug treatment center)
6. Abandonment by and of friends
7. Depletion of economic resources due to drug use
8. Client's level of motivation
9. Client's evaluation of the need for treatment
10. Therapist's ratings indicating a need for treatment for this modality

■ **Modality V—Acceptance.** Ideally, when the client has progressed to the level of acceptance, he or she accepts responsibility for the inability to effectively control the use of drugs. In other words, a breakdown in the level of denial occurs. Now the clinician should investigate:

1. Client's belief that there is a need for assistance in eliminating drug usage
2. Increased levels of anxiety concerning drug dependency
3. Increased feelings of vulnerability and helplessness over the effect(s) of drugs
4. Increased psychomotor retardation and agitation
5. Client's level of motivation
6. Client's evaluation of the need for treatment
7. Ratings indicating a need for treatment for this modality

■ **Modality VI—Resolution.** At this stage, the clinician and client begin to find answers to the issues and problems related to the substance-related disorder. Now is the time for a full analysis of the problem of concern, assuming that the dynamics of the other modalities have been properly identified and evaluated.

The clinician reviews and determines if the overall assessment has addressed the following areas of concern. (If not, the clinician returns to the area in question and reassesses the problem or issue.)

1. Results of a mental status examination (including suicide and violence potential)
2. Client's presenting problem(s)
3. Client's behavioral orientation
4. Level (severity of duration) of disruption of the client's functioning
5. Antecedent events

6. The who and/or what is /are sustaining the problem(s).
7. What the client needs to change and how the change can be accomplished
8. Client's strengths and weaknesses
9. Other treatment(s) the client has undergone and the results

   Subsequent to assessment in this modality, the therapist develops a treatment plan. The treatment plan should, of course, take into account all of the modality assessments. The data gathered should explain the drug abuse/dependency problems at the current level of understanding, and a formal diagnosis should then be made.

■ **Modality VII—Entry.** See the following section for a discussion of the Entry Declatype as it relates to the post-treatment phase of therapy.

Further Testing.   In the event that an impasse occurs during any phase of treatment, the clinician should consider performing a Higher Ordered Modality Profile Evaluation (HOMPE). (See relevant discussion of higher-ordered conditioning in Lazarus, 1981.) The second, higher-ordered, Modality Profile evaluation HOMPE provides, consists of subjecting any problem on the Modality Profile to a more detailed examination. In the event that an impasse still exists, the clinician may consider conducting a third HOMPE. Some clinicians, however, may also want to resort to the use of various standardized tests and/or other psychological instruments (where appropriate) to gather additional information.

Post-Treatment

During the post-treatment phase of DECLARE Therapy, the primary emphasis is on aftercare and recovery issues.

   The client is ready for Entry when he or she has achieved disengagement (at least 90 days of complete abstinence) from the world of drug abuse and is entering/reentering conventional society, where drug abuse has no proper place. The major goals of this modality are to assist the client in:

■ Avoiding some of the most common, and often predictable, social/psychological "hemorrhaging" factors producing relapse
■ Developing a reasonably comfortable and satisfactory lifestyle enhanced by a sense of freedom from the downward spiral of drug abuse

Part of the Entry phase involves the assessment of the person's readiness to return to the world he or she left, and part of the returning to this "real world" involves the recognition and awareness that this world is full of challenges, some of which participated in the individual's disease process. Some of the challenges may involve subtle biopsychosocial factors such as craving, resentment, comorbidity, anger, poor social relations, mood changes, lack of meaningful support and a dearth of sobriety-maintaining leisure-time activities.

By putting adequate emphasis on aftercare and recovery, clinicians can reduce recidivism and enhance rehabilitation, enabling the client to return to a community that is supportive of growth and accomplishment, rather than to an environment that perpetuates problem behavior. In its aftercare/recovery approach, DECLARE Therapy advocates exploring new avenues designed to move beyond the more traditional modes of service delivery.

Stages and Warning Signs of Relapse

In order to prevent relapse or psychosocial hemorrhage, it is important to emphasize to the client the necessity of self-monitoring on a daily basis and encourage, for self-monitoring purposes, use of the Biphasic Analysis Reintegration Sequence, or BARS, form. The BARS format represents two separate phases:

1. Demonstrated disengagement from the world of drug abuse, i.e., complete abstinence from drug use
2. Maintenance of therapeutic gains through appropriate aftercare/recovery, which facilitates one's sense of personal empowerment, e.g., self-monitoring

Phase 1.   In phase 1 of the stage, it is important to assist the client in anticipating the occurrence of strong urges and cravings for drugs which may appear quite suddenly and unexpectedly. The client should be forewarned that these urges may be triggered by environmental and/or psychological stimuli—that is, people, places, objects, and/or situations that have been previously associated with drugs. Even various internal states, such as love, depression, hunger, stress, success, anxiety, fatigue, boredom, may trigger drug use. Therefore, unless pre-warned and educated, the client may erroneously conclude from the strength of the urge signals that the treatment process is no longer effective, a false assumption that could lead the client to impulsively terminate any previously learned skills and to return to an NBO style of behavior.

Obviously, all clients should be educated to understand that once a craving begins, it will not inevitably grow in intensity until it can no longer be resisted. Instead, it should be emphasized to the client that the cravings generally reach a peak within one to three hours and, in most cases, then subside. Whenever cravings (or any other signs of relapse) occur, the person should take immediate, helpful action. It is critical, in fact, that clients learn how to attend to the earliest warning signs of potential relapse so that they may initiate appropriate action (see Chapter 5).

Early recognition of potential relapse is, of course, crucial, for if the situation is permitted to deteriorate to disastrous proportions, it is extremely difficult to do anything about it. Aware of the importance of immediate action, one client suggested a "four-second rule." He felt that he must react within four seconds of exposure if he were to diminish his threat. When taking quick action (through such techniques as thought-stopping, distractions, and seeking the company of nonusing friends) a person can nullify a return to an NBO style of behavior and drug use.

Clients who are headed for relapse will commonly engage in a series of self-destructive behaviors (NBO) that precede impending drug abuse. These behaviors include such activities as:

- Reuniting with former drug-abusing friends
- Harboring negative thoughts, feelings, frustrations, resentments, and fears
- Allowing warning signs to go unattended
- Frequenting places where previous drug-abusing behavior has occurred
- Isolating oneself

It is vital that the clinician and client spot these potential warning signs so that appropriate action can be initiated. To that goal, the following suggestions are offered to help facilitate relapse prevention.

Basically, the appropriate actions can be facilitated by regular and consistent use of the BARS form, which, as mentioned earlier, can be one of the client's most effective tools for effective aftercare. On the BARS form, the client can keep a daily record of efforts to remain drug free, an exercise than can be extremely reinforcing.

Using the BARS Form.   The use of the BARS form is quite simple. The client is asked to be aware of the common types of warning signs listed at the bottom of the form and to check off each one if and when they occur. (Clients may also add their own warning signs if they choose.) The client is then asked to record what he or she did in response to these signs.

On a daily basis, at bedtime, the client is also required to select five non-drug-related activities (from the reinforcement menu) to perform the next day—activities designed to provide pleasure. The next day, the client keeps track of these activities by noting them in the large spaces in the columns provided.

In addition, the clinician should encourage the client to list each day's activities on a scale of 1 to 10. Ideally, the client records and rates activities weekly and then rates the week (using the same scale) and charts it on the Declagram of Well-Being. This exercise helps the client and clinician to separate reality from illusion.

Phase 2.   Phase 2 of the aftercare process begins after the first year of sobriety and continues for the rest of the individual's life. Treatment during this phase may include continued individual therapy and/or group participation. The major goal of the second phase is to maintain therapeutic gains through continued aftercare and maintenance of a PBO.

Some of the major tasks for the client to be aware of during this period are:

- The challenge of establishing an awareness of his or her support network
- Overconfidence—i.e., testing controls
- Denial
- Loss of esteem
- Confusion

■ Loss of Significant Resources
■ Flare-ups
■ Issues regarding development (education, children, etc.)
■ Acceptance of self
■ Reclaiming an NBO

The Case of M.K.

Substance Abuse History.   M.K. is a 26-year-old, white female, self-referred following the breakup with her boyfriend (which resulted from an argument over her drug use). The initial structured screening indicates that she is a polydrug abuser, as evidenced by positive drug urine screening for cocaine, barbiturates, and marijuana. M.K. related a thirteen-year history (dating to preadolescence) of polydrug abuse, including hallucinogens, alcohol, heroin, barbiturates, and cocaine.

The client reports that at age 13 she began gradually to abuse alcohol (which she currently drinks to excess, at least three days per week). She also reports that during the past thirteen years she at one time smoked marijuana daily; has occasionally used LSD, MDA, psilocybin, and barbiturates; and injected heroin once.

M.K. says her drug of choice is now cocaine, which she has used on a daily basis for the past two years. Initially, she consumed cocaine (snorted) once or twice a week in amounts of one-quarter gram, she says. She now reports using approximately two to two-and-one-half grams of cocaine per week.

The client also has a history of somatic complaints, depression, and anxiety, which predate her substance abuse. After two weeks of complete abstinence, as evidenced by the urine screening, she was administered the following instruments.

Tests Administered.   In determining M.K.'s level of functioning, the following assessment instruments were administered: Taylor Historical Questionnaire–Revised (THQ-R); Multifaceted Assessment of Chemical Dependency Inventory–Revised (MAC-D-R); Wechsler Adult Intelligence Scale–Revised (WAIS-R); House-Tree-Person; Bender Gestalt; Draw-A-Person-In-The-Rain Anxiety Scale–Revised (DAPIR-R); Beck Depression Scale; and the Rorschach Test.

Test Behavior.   M.K. was evaluated at a counseling center. Dressed in jeans, shirt, and sneakers, her affect appeared depressed and anxious concerning her presenting problems. Rapport, however, was quickly established, with her exhibiting the type of reserve expected in a new situation. She did well in highly structured situations, which allowed her to focus her energy on a specific task.

The client seemed to want to answer the questions correctly and was reluctant to give up on any of the questions. She was cooperative during the testing session; and she appeared to be motivated to do well.

Intellectual Functioning.   Test results indicated that M.K. was functioning in the "normal" range of intelligence. There were no noted deficits in general information (factual knowledge), arithmetic (the ability to analyze a given set of material and then to recognize the elements needed for solving a specific problem), object assembly, inductive reasoning, perceptual organization, and spatial visualization ability.

On the WAIS-R, M.K. achieved a verbal scale IQ of 94, a performance scale IQ of 104 and a full scale score of 98, placing her in the previously mentioned "normal" range of intellectual ability. The present measure of intellectual functioning appears to be valid. Results of perceptual-motor testing (Bender) also indicate normal performance. M.K. did not exhibit any distortions in shape, rotating, and/or integration difficulties. Results of the Beck Depression Scale indicated a moderate level of depression.

Personality Functioning. M.K. presents a consistent pattern of a very anxious and insecure adult. Behavioral observations, test results, and verbal reports indicate that anxiety and low self-esteem are significantly impairing her emotional, social, and academic functioning.

Integrating the above findings with projective testing indicated the presence of depression and anxiety. Results further indicated a consistent pattern of emotional poverty, isolation, and immaturity—suggesting a lack of social contact and involvement with other people. These findings are not inconsistent with drug-abusing individuals.

M.K. displayed a vague, fluid response style. "Playing it safe" appeared to be her method of coping with her lack of self-confidence. There was an emphasis on affective output, which may be indicative of poor impulse control. The results of reality testing were intact, and her abstracting and integrating abilities were adequate. She was oriented in time, place, person, and situation, and there were no signs of any previous mental and/or emotional disorders.

Test results showed a notable lack of genuine human contact in the Rorschach. This may be suggestive of a lack of real involvement with other people, a finding supported by her present lifestyle.

Verbal reports indicate that she perceives most people in her environment as "phony." Currently, she has few friends, and so consequently, she has few outlets for expression of feelings. She thus engages in drug-abusing behavior as a means of coping. This results in periods of depression and self-deprecation.

Education, Vocation, Financial Situation. M.K. is a high school graduate who has completed two years of college at a state university. Her major was psychology. After dropping out of college for a brief time, she found employment as a waitress in a local restaurant. She was never successful in this position, however, and terminated her employment after working in several different restaurants.

M.K. does not have any clear vocational objectives at the present time, and she seems to lack any confidence in being successful (regarding a vocation) in the future. She has expressed an interest in eventually returning to school full time "some day" to complete her bachelor's degree.

The client is financially dependent on her father and stepmother, with whom she lives. Her mother, a nurse, lives out of state. She has financed her addiction by receiving drugs as payment for being a "mule" (a person who carries drugs in and/or out of an area) and from borrowing money from family members. M.K. feels alone and lacks meaningful personal relationships.

Legal.   M.K. has never been involved with the criminal justice system regarding her drugs and/or any other situations.

Social History.   M.K. states that the majority of her using social contacts are in the "drug scene" (like her), and some are "either in jail or dead." She also indicates that she has few "straight" social contacts. The client admits that she does not have any non-drug-related social and/or recreational activities; and she says when she is not engaged in drug-taking behavior, she is bored. Prior to her current social isolation and heavy involvement ($60/day) in a drug-abusing lifestyle, she enjoyed swimming, running, biking, and listening to jazz.

Physical History.   M.K's physical history is unremarkable excerpt for recurrent headaches, which at times are very intense. She also reports that she has never been hospitalized for any medical problems. Neither has she ever been hospitalized for any drug-related problems such as overdose, withdrawal, and/or detoxification. She presents no significant health condition(s) or handicap(s) that would affect treatment.

Treatment History.   M.K. has no prior history of treatment for drug abuse or alcoholism. Neither has she had any type of counseling or psychotherapy for any mental or emotional disorder(s).

Initial Modality Profile.   In view of this case history, it is interesting to look at M.K.'s initial Modality Profile, which was constructed during the assessment phase of her evaluation for substance abuse.

Denial.   Anger; hurt feelings; resistance; passivity.

Esteem.   Majority of social contacts in the "drug scene"; few "straight" friends; poor self-image; implications that she feels fat; impaired social relationships; lack of success; depression; self-blame; few outlets for self-expression; lack of self-respect; immaturity; anxiety.

Confusion.   Anxious; insecure, withdrawn; poor impulse control; continued drug use; depression; low frustration tolerance; life controlled by outside forces; inability to cope.

Loss.   Unsuccessful in employment; unclear vocational objectives; physical complaints (headaches); decreased libido; estranged from boyfriend.

Acceptance.   Believes there is a problem; wants some help; says it hurts to be this way; does not know what to do; feels helpless.

Resolution. Has doubts about therapy; desires more control in her life; wants to get better, shows increased motivation to be drug free; desires more information on drug abuse education; wants to define her problems; exhibits impaired problem-solving ability and poor decision making; wants to feel better; wants to get rid of anxiety.

Entry. Lacks support system; has no long-term goals; lacks self-respect, direction in life, and appropriate leisure activities.

Summary. M.K. presents a picture of a very verbal individual with "normal" intellectual ability, multiple psychological problems, and a limited support system.

There is considerable interpersonal conflict, which is reinforced by her continued drug-taking behavior. Her emotional problems include poor self-image, depression, and anxiety. She lacks success in her life and has a recurring pattern of drug-abusing behavior used to cope with stress.

M.K.'s lack of success in interpersonal relationships has reinforced her depression and poor self-concept. As previously indicated, she lacks emotional support from significant others and feels isolated. Her present symptoms include dysphoric mood, lack of interest in pleasurable activities, poor appetite, somatic complaints, irritability, and anxiety.

Her thirteen-year history of drug abuse appears to represent an attempt to cope with stress and anxiety to alleviate her psychological problems.

Diagnosis.

Axis I:	304.20; Cocaine dependence, moderate; partial remission
Axis II:	Diagnosis deferred
Axis III:	Severe headaches
Axis IV:	Psychosocial stressor: breakup with boyfriend; mild 2 (predominantly acute event)
Axis V:	Current GAF, 60; highest GAF, past year, 75

Treatment Plan.   Considering the scope of M.K's problems, it was mutually agreed that treatment would be multifaceted and include the following:

1. Complete abstinence from all mood-altering substances except those professionally prescribed for medical purposes. She was required to provide urine samples randomly.
2. A complete medical examination to determine if there has been any physical impact as a result of her dependence on drugs.
3. Counseling to determine and to resolve Declatypes as well as any entopsychic problems or conflicts and to improve social support, maximize emotional competencies, and seek to develop appropriate non-chemical-coping mechanisms.

Counseling should also facilitate the emotional and intellectual understanding of the sources of current difficulties. M.K. is a good candidate for counseling because she is highly motivated to change old attitudes and behavior, and she is capable of following through with a therapeutic treatment regime.

4. Relaxation training and behavior modification to assist her in tension reduction and in better coping with the anxieties of daily life.
5. The development of a social support system to strengthen her currently limited social network. It was thought that by becoming involved in NA and similar groups, she might find appropriate peer support. It was also suggested that she become involved with an activity therapy group to develop appropriate outlets for leisure time.
6. Vocational counseling to clarify vocational goals and objectives and to assist her in developing a realistic educational and/or job development program.
7. Psychiatric consultation to determine if her depression requires medical management.
8. Drug education via seminars, lectures, books, articles, and films to assist her in developing a better understanding of the medical consequences of using drugs of abuse and to encourage her to view her personal choices about drugs and alcohol within the framework of individual responsibility.

Course of Treatment.   The various therapeutic goals utilized with this client included cognitive behavioral approach, urine analysis, relaxation, social services, and vocational counseling. The rationale includes:

1. Drug education—to develop an understanding of (a) the medical consequences of abusing drugs and alcohol and (b) drug/alcohol and personal responsibility
2. Urine analysis—to determine the physical presence of drugs
3. Counseling—to focus on abstinence and on her need to abuse drugs to cope with interpersonal and entopsychic problems
4. Social services—to develop a positive, drug-free support system
5. Vocational rehabilitation—to develop more realistic educational/job goals and development
6. Relaxation—to reduce tension
7. Psychiatric consultation—to medically manage depression
8. Medical examination—to determine the origins of her severe headaches

Discharge Summary.   M.K. accepted the treatment plan. During the initial four months of treatment she attended, with few exceptions, all her individual and group sessions. On several occasions while in treatment, she expressed feelings of anxiety, depression, and resentment. Upon evaluation by a psychiatrist it was determined that she required no medical intervention to manage her depression.

On a number of occasions, she expressed reservations—i.e., "Will I ever get any better?" Despite reservation, she continued to follow through on assignments and attended sessions on a regular basis.

During this period of her treatment, M.K. was given an exercise program (of running, swimming, and bicycling) to follow. She initially followed through with the program, but expressed some difficulty in completing the requirements of training. Throughout this period she was given routine drug (urine) screening evaluations and was consistently found to be drug free.

At one point during her treatment period, she reapplied to college for full-time classes and was accepted. Approximately eight weeks later she abruptly dropped out of treatment (against the advice of her therapist) to accept employment out-of-state. Several months later M.K. contacted her former counselor and reported that she has remained drug free and is attending support group meetings on a regular basis.

The Case of W.R.

Note: A Modality Profile can be developed with emphasis on one or more of the Declatypes. The following case demonstrates the development of a Modality Profile with emphasis on denial.

W.R. is a 34-year-old married, black male referred by the courts for child abuse. In this case the courts requested a substance abuse assessment and a psychological examination as part of a custody hearing involving his three children. Follow-up, however, was impossible because the client fled the jurisdiction of the court and his whereabouts remain unknown.

Initial Evaluation. W.R. arrived for evaluation at the appropriate time. Upon his arrival, however, he indicated that he was "on probation and was ordered by the court to have some testing performed." He was confused regarding who was going to conduct the evaluation; but later, accepted the circumstances and dropped any suspicious attitude he originally had toward the examiner. He was, in fact, cooperative during the entire evaluation.

W.R. was dressed in slacks, shirt, and sneakers. He maintained eye contact with the examiner during the interview and seemed almost cheerful, but anxious. W.R. was oriented times three (for time, place, and person) and there were no unusual disturbances in speech and/or thought content.

Tests Administered. The client was given the following tests: Rorschach Test; Minnesota Multiphasic Personality Inventory (MMPI-2); IPAT (anxiety test); Mental Status Examination; Taylor Historical Questionnaire–Revised (THQ-R); Hand Test.

Assessment Results and Clinical Impressions. Thematically, the patterns on the Rorschach support a picture of an individual who is aggressive and preoccupied with sexual fantasies that appear to be marginally repressed. Rorschach results also indicate a personality that is demanding and that has a weak adaptive style in interpersonal relationships.

W.R. does not carefully consider decisions and often reacts without adequate evaluation, judgment, and inhibitions. Content analysis of the Rorschach indicates that he alternates between projection (blaming others), introjection (blaming self), and denial (refusal to believe that something has happened). Consequently, his judgment, understanding, and problem-solving skills are unreliable to meet life's demands—i.e., parenting, working, and social life.

On the MMPI-2, W.R. responded to items consistently. He presented himself as adequate (in terms of social relationships) and well adjusted, denying common human shortcomings in an unsophisticated attempt to present himself in the best possible light. Results further suggest an angry, immature person who outwardly tends to be a conformist but who really discharges his hostile, rebellious feelings in indirect ways.

He wishes to be dependent, but also wishes to be independent, and typically vacillates angrily between the two. He tends to engage in marginal relationships with other acting-out-type individuals, thereby vicariously gratifying his own antisocial tendencies.

The client's pattern of responses suggests fertile soil for dissociative phenomena frequently associated with alcoholism. Results further indicate some psychosocial problems, including marital disharmony and sexual promiscuity. He displays poor judgment under stress, and emotional outbursts may be only minimally related to their provocation. His profile indicates cyclic patterns of violent outbursts with intermittent periods of appropriate behavior. This represents a stable personality disorder that is extremely difficult to change.

The Hand Test (a diagnostic technique consisting of ten cards using hands as a projective medium) was administered in the hope that it might contribute something additional toward the final evaluation of the client. Test results revealed a conglomeration of dysfunctional signs. His responses to cards II and V, for instance, have a bizarre flavor. The results of this test also indicated a highly aggressive, dysfunctional personality type who has a high probability of behaving in an overt, hostile, antisocial manner. These results are particularly interesting because they seem to accurately reflect the mixed state of this individual's dysfunctional thoughts, affects, and behaviors, as well as the crude, aggressive responses that are sometimes expressed in his overt behavior.

Results of the IPAT anxiety test indicate "normal" levels of anxiety, which seem to contradict other findings. Perhaps this may be best explained by this individual's extreme efforts to present himself in the best possible light. Results of the Mental Status Examinations were consistent with other findings.

Results of the THQ-R indicate a seventeen-year history of drug abuse. At age 17, W. R. began to gradually abuse alcohol, which he currently drinks to excess several days a week. He also reports that he has used heroin and cocaine intravenously and that six years ago, he was hospitalized with a fungus infection in his right lung—the result of intravenous drug use. He also reports currently abusing his prescription drug (Tylenol with codeine) and alcohol (80 oz. per day) until the former is exhausted.

Assessment further reveals that he has experienced at least eight separate occasions of drug overdose. Currently, he indicates spending only fifty dollars per month on drugs. In light of his past history of drug abuse, this information regarding the cost of drugs was viewed cautiously.

W.R. also reports having engaged in illegal activities for profit during the past thirty days. He was unwilling, however, to indicate the extent of these illegal activities.

It is important to note that he does not regard himself as being an alcoholic and/or drug dependent (state of denial). He says that he abuses drugs to "relax or unwind," "feel adequate," "be less critical of himself," "feel more accepted by others," "avoid things," "get to sleep" and/or "think." He also states that he uses drugs when he is angry, depressed, worried, tired, or lonely.

This behavior also represents his alternating between projection (blaming others), introjection (blaming self), and denial (refusal to believe that something has happened). His seventeen-year history of drug abuse appears to represent an attempt to cope with anxiety and depression and to alleviate his emotional problems. His inability to cope effectively, notwithstanding his responses, dynamically represent a chronic pattern of alternating between blaming others or self and denying the seriousness of his present situation and problems.

Initial Modality Profile

Following is the Modality Profile that was completed for W.R. after his initial evaluation. Unfortunately, it was impossible to complete the assessment process and to develop a treatment plan for this client because he violated the conditions of his probation. As we shall see, however, even with limited information, the Modality Profile may still serve as a starting point in the initial development of a treatment plan and prove helpful in selecting appropriate techniques for later intervention.

Denial. Insists, "I am not drug dependent"; uses drugs to unwind, to relax, to avoid things.

Esteem. To feel adequate; to feel less critical of self; to feel more accepted by others; anxiety; lack of motivation; blames others; anger; aggression.

Confusion. Worried; angry; sleep problems; numerous overdoses; suspiciousness; blames others for problems; repeated negative consequences from drug abuse.

Loss. Job; health problems; marital discord; parenting difficulties; psychological problems; probation; disorganized lifestyle; limits set by legal authority; need of examiner's assistance to get children back.

Acceptance. The con; attempts to appear better than he is.

Resolution. Absence of motivation to seek treatment on his own.

Entry. Lacks social support system; continuous relationship with drug-abusing friends; currently engaged in illegal activities (drug related); no vocational goals; lacks stable positive relationships; poor problem-solving skills; negative living arrangement; continued drug/alcohol abuse.

Diagnosis.   Given the above test results and clinical impressions, the following appears appropriate:

Axis I: 304.90; Polysubstance Dependence V61.20; Parent/child problems

Axis II: 301.83; Borderline Personality Disorder (provisional)

Axis III: Asthma

Axis IV: Psychosocial stresses: probation; parenting and marital discord severity; 3 moderate (predominantly enduring circumstances)

Axis V: Current GAF, 40; highest GAF, 50

Potential Treatment Plan

As previously noted, it was impossible to develop a treatment plan for this client. Had he accepted treatment, however, the following plan would have been suggested, based on current information. (It is important to keep in mind that a plan developed without input from the client is generally not as successful as a plan developed with the client's input.)

Considering the scope of W.R.'s problems, a treatment plan would include detoxification and, later, complete abstinence from drugs (except those prescribed by a physician for specific medical purposes). The client would also be taken under supervision and would be required to provide random urine samples. In conjunction with all this, W.R. would receive a complete physical examination to determine the extent of his physical impairment.

After at least two weeks (or more if possible) of complete abstinence, another psychological examination would be conducted and comparisons would be made with earlier results. This information would be useful in determining the degree of psychological impairment present. Keep in mind that the results of previous psychological testing should be cautiously interpreted due to the influence of drugs on the client's responses.

It would also be recommended to W.R. that he attend both individual and group therapy sessions to improve social support, to maximize emotional competency, and to assist in the development of appropriate nonchemical coping mechanisms. Counseling would, ideally, facilitate emotional and intellectual understanding regarding the sources of the client's current difficulties.

In addition, a program involving social services would be strongly encouraged to strengthen W.R.'s limited support system. Vocational rehabilitation, too, should be employed to clarify for the client his vocational objectives and to develop a realistic job development program. Intensive drug education, too, should be employed to assist W.R. in developing drug/alcohol understanding and to manage denial. This would allow him to view personal choices about drugs/alcohol within a framework of individual responsibility that is congruent with traditional values, beliefs, and personal attitudes.

Recapping . . .

■ In DECLARE Therapy, the therapist's diagnostic impressions and ratings define the need for and the course of treatment.

■ An effective treatment plan is based on reports of the amount, duration, and intensity of signs and symptoms within the specific DECLARE modality considered.

■ DECLARE Therapy presents specific procedures for gathering information during the initial interview. The procedures require a description of the assessment and diagnosis for each modality.

■ Essential to this phase of the DECLARE program are clinician ratings and client ratings, the development of a Modality Profile, and a *declaration* of the goals and objectives of both client and clinician.

■ DECLARE Therapy offers a number of tools useful in assessment, diagnosis, and treatment planning, including the Taylor Historical Questionnaire–Revised (THQ-R), the MAC-D Inventory–Revised (MAC-D-R), and the BARS form.

CHAPTER

5   Challenges and Choices

Recovery is a journey—a journey that takes time. No one can recover without the willingness to face challenges and to make choices. The journey, then, consists of:

- Meeting challenges
- Making choices
- Experiencing the joy of a new life

That's the good news. The bad news is that most individuals find it difficult to understand that, like addiction, recovery is a journey and not a quick fix. Anyone who has ever attempted to recover from an addiction realizes that traveling that road leading to a new life is far from easy. Challenges are plentiful.

There are moments when the client feels able to conquer the world and handle any challenges that present themselves. Then there are times when recovery just doesn't seem worth the effort. Some clients, in fact, report feeling discouraged when they enter the recovery phase.

Most individuals automatically assume that abstinence alone is the prerequisite for recovery. In reality, abstinence is not the only criterion. The act of recovery involves completing a series of daily tasks that allow the management of both acute withdrawal and postwithdrawal while simultaneously correcting the biopsychosocial damage resulting from years of abuse.

For every challenge the client faces, there exists a corresponding choice. A recovering addict may choose to deal with the challenge(s) in a way that supports the desire to maintain sobriety or in a way that places the recovery process at risk. Though difficult at times, recovery is possible.

This concluding chapter examines the common challenges encountered by clients on the journey to full recovery. It also describes a simple recovery-supporting process based on the DECLARE acronym.

Managing Recovery Challenges

Essentially, recovery challenges are the obstacles that prevent the client from maintaining sobriety. Recovery challenges include but are not limited to:

- Unexpected changes resulting from sobriety
- Decreased motivation
- Drinking/drugging when feeling happy, hungry, sad, hopeful, stressed, angry, and/or depressed
- Relapses
- Absence of support from family, friends, and business associates

These challenges vary. In other words, what is a challenge for one person is not necessarily a challenge for another. Also, what appears as a challenge in one situation may not necessarily be a challenge in another.

In addressing the challenges of successful recovery, DECLARE Therapy presents a seven-step program whereby the clinician encourages the client to:

D. Decide if he/she wants to recover
E. Establish a challenge checklist
C. Choose what works for the individual
L. Lose the fear of recovery
A. Act upon the plan that has been established
R. Record results
E. Evaluate results

Let's explore each step in depth.

Decide: What Is Your Most Immediate Challenge?

To avoid being overwhelmed, clients in the recovery phase of therapy should focus on the immediate challenge facing them. Initially the clinician is responsible for keeping the client focused on the "here and now." To this end, every effort should be made to instill confidence. Clients should be encouraged to take small steps, one (second, minute, hour, day) at a time. And one challenge at a time. That's how it's done!

Clients in the recovery phase of therapy should be coaxed to ask themselves, "What is my most immediate recovery challenge? What is most likely to cause me to use again today?" In other words, clients need to focus *all* their energy on one specific challenge at a time.

Commonly, the most immediate challenge facing the client is disassociation from old friends or associates. Every time he or she runs into an old drug-using friend, the reaction is, "Come on, man. You're not much fun these days. Lighten up and relax a little. . . . Just have one more hit. . . . If you don't like it, then don't use anymore. . . . Let's get this 8-ball. . . . Let's get this bottle . . ." Clients must recognize the threat such encounters pose. How they respond to them will determine their future success.

Establish a Challenge Checklist

Clients should be encouraged to develop a checklist of all the possible challenges they will face when they enter/reenter society. After listing these challenges, they should rank them according to their immediacy. They should then be urged to handle the most immediate challenge first.

Articulating challenges by writing them down is one of the most important steps in the recovery process. The clinician should guide the client in establishing a checklist at the appropriate time. Through repeated practice, it becomes second nature to use the checklist after therapy has been completed.

Choose What Works

Next the clinician should assist clients in developing strategies that work. Because many clients have difficulty in making important changes in their lives, the clinician must be willing to explore every possible avenue to determine what can and cannot work.

Clients should be encouraged to attend community support group meetings such as AA, NA, CA, and so forth, to gather ideas on how others have been successful in maintaining their recovery. They should also be reminded of the many recovery skills learned in therapy and encouraged to use them. Finally, clients should maintain their BARS forms. Outlining activities helps in building self-reliance and reminds the client of workable strategies.

Lose the Fear of Recovery

Many clients are fearful of the recovery process. Why is this? It is because they must now live without what has dominated their life for a long time. They are afraid to live without the god, friend, or lover that has given them pleasure and companionship, taken away fear, and given them vital confidence. No wonder there is so much fear!

As therapists, we must recognize this fear in our clients and must never allow it to paralyze them into inaction. Instead, we must empower them with the knowledge that recovery is worth all the effort they have to expend, reminding them that life was far from perfect when they were using drugs and alcohol.

What can we clinicians do to facilitate our clients' loss of fear regarding recovery? The answer to this question is as diverse as the clients we treat, because each client is different. However, here are some ideas that seem to work for a majority of clients.

We can, for example, help clients to compare and contrast the way they used to be with how they are today by taking a photo of the client at the beginning of treatment and showing it to them periodically. We can remind them that what they were doing before did not work.

We may ask them why they decided to become sober in the first place. Their responses will include the negatives associated with being out of control—loss of self-respect and self-esteem, loss of trust from family members, going to jail or prison, being sick, having problems with memory, and so forth. All of these can be reasons to fear not being sober more than fearing sobriety. For whatever reasons, the choice is the client's.

Act Upon the Plan

Clients should understand that what works for them in one situation may not work in another. Of course, finding out what works is a matter of trial and error. Should a certain tactic not work the first time, clients should be encouraged to keep trying until they find one that does. Remember, for both the client and the therapist, recovery is a journey, and like any journey, we sometimes make the wrong turn. We do, however, generally get back on the correct path and eventually arrive at our destination.

Record Results

As we have seen throughout the text (see esp. Chapter 4), the BARS self-monitoring scale constitutes a simple and effective method for recording results. It is in fact one of the most valuable recovery tools available to the client. The BARS form allows clients to keep track of the daily challenges and the choices faced in avoiding the substances of abuse and maintaining therapeutic goals. The BARS form is especially effective when used in combination with the challenge checklist, described earlier.

Evaluate Results

Only the client can truly judge whether he or she has been successful in dealing with a challenge. In making such an evaluation, the client should review the BARS form to assess the satisfaction level of the results. All clients in recovery should ask themselves the following questions:

- Was I able to follow my daily/weekly plan and meet my challenge to not use again?
- What did I do today that worked?
- How do I feel about myself today?

Using the DECLARE seven-step process can help clients deal with whatever challenges they may face. Remember, challenges change over time. Today's challenge may not be tomorrow's, or it may remain a challenge for very different reasons. It is vital that clinicians encourage clients to do whatever is necessary to maintain their recovery and to feel good about their efforts to be both successful and happy.

Motivation

Motivation refers to a driving force that moves us to a particular action. For example, certain behaviors are likely to help us obtain success, pleasure, the next meal, the next drink of water, and so on. However, at times we lose motivation when our behaviors are not reinforced. The lack of reinforcement discourages purposeful activity, which further reduces reinforcement. Clients, therefore, must prevent their level of motivation from falling below a certain point.

The following sections suggest methods for helping clients stay motivated in their quest for sobriety.

Recall the Reason Why

Among addicts and alcoholics, there is a tendency after a period of recovery to think, "Now I know how to drink or use socially," "I can handle it now," "I have enough discipline now," "I just need to think this through and decide how I will quit." This is very dangerous thinking, of course, because it usually leads to disaster. At this point clients must remind themselves of the reasons they were motivated to stop using drugs or alcohol in the first place. The first four Declatypes provide the answer.

1. **Denial.** Remind clients that they once denied even having a problem—in spite of everything they did, the people they hurt and the danger in which they put themselves. This pattern of denial breeds isolation and alienation of the self and ultimately leads to the resumption of use.
2. **Esteem.** Remind clients how they felt about themselves when they were using—how difficult it was to go home after being out for seven days, drinking and/or drugging; how other people in the neighborhood did not respect them. Remind them how they felt when people thought they were in the way and treated them like a piece of furniture. Ask them how they felt when their children asked for school money and the embarrassment they felt inside about why they couldn't give it to them. Ask them to recall the feelings of shame, remorse, guilt, and the suicidal ideations they felt resulting from their use.
3. **Confusion.** Remind clients how out of control and totally unmanageable their lives were as a result of drugs and alcohol.
4. **Loss.** Remind clients of all the things that drugs and/or alcohol caused them to lose. These comments from a client tell the story:

> I lost my job, lost my family. I just lost everything I had. I lost it . . . I lost control of myself, whatever alcohol can do . . . it can take everything you got and more. I lost my self-respect . . . I lost that . . . I just lost everything I had . . . especially my family . . . that hurts the most and I really lost my son, who is now 10 years old.

Clients must be discouraged from attempting to remember only the good times about their drinking/drugging. They should be reminded, in great detail, about what it was really like. They should also be reminded that they never want to be that kind of person again. A useful technique in this regard is to ask clients to write down the reasons why they decided to stop using. They should then place this list where they will see it often—on the bathroom wall, on the refrigerator, or in a hallway, for example. In this way, each time they begin to wonder, "Why am I in recovery?" they can see why at a glance.

Rethinking Sobriety

During the course of recovery, there are times when clients will express concerns about being in a motivational slump. This typically occurs after a considerable time of sobriety. Sometimes, for instance, clients will say, "I was just planning to stay sober until I got off probation."

Whenever clients get off probation, they need to make an important decision by asking themselves, "Do I continue to stay in recovery?" If the answer to that crucial question is yes, they may need to find new reasons to stay in recovery. So the new question becomes, "Why do I need sobriety at this time?"

The clinician can help clients to answer this question in light of their current life situation. In addition, the clinician may ask, "Don't you feel better now?" Or, "Have you taken a look at yourself these days? Don't you look great, compared to the way you looked a year ago?"

Reassessing Choices

In the course of a client's recovery program, certain challenges may cause the client to want to use again. The most helpful approach to this problem is to have the client reassess his or her choices in response to a particularly difficult challenge.

Recovery is a process that requires constant evaluation and reevaluation. Productive assessment serves to enhance clients' PBOs and may result, for example, in their attending more meetings, changing environments, changing friends, and even seeking additional counseling.

Client Recovery Expectations

Recovering alcoholics and addicts often have unrealistic expectations about recovery. They mistakenly think all they have to do is just STOP using and their lives will be just fine. Needless to say, if they expect that this is all there is to it, they will be frustrated and disappointed until they eventually relapse. At this point, client motivation generally decreases sharply. To assist clients with their expectations, therefore, the process must be put in perspective. Here are two suggestions that should help.

■ Encourage clients to stop the "stinking thinking"—the negative thoughts, that is, NBO. Remind clients that whenever obsessive and intrusive thoughts about using drugs and alcohol enter their thoughts, they should subvocally scream, "STOP IT!" over and over again. Clients can be encouraged to visualize a stop sign or a flashing stop light to aid in this process. This method, in combination with relaxation exercises, has been reported by many clients to be most effective in halting negative thought patterns.

■ Ask clients to verbalize an answer to the question, "What is my life like today?" If necessary, require them to write down an answer. This generally adds considerable reality to their evaluation. Then ask them to tell you (or write down) the answer to this question: "What will my life be like in six months if I use again?" Remind them that they must learn to cope with life. Whenever this is effectively accomplished, they will have developed the knowledge and the skill necessary to maintain their recovery.

Developing Incentives

We know that addicts and alcoholics have a difficult time sustaining recovery. As clinicians, we are well aware of the demands these people face in maintaining their sobriety. We are also aware that to sustain their motivation, clients must be provided with appropriate incentives. Changing or modifying incentives can break up the arduous task of recovery into smaller pieces, thus making the long and challenging journey of recovery easier to undertake.

Clients should be encouraged to develop an incentives checklist dealing with specific recovery challenges. This could include specific goals in problem areas such as controlling temper, anger, remorse; handling embarrassment; maintaining family support; dealing with guilt feelings; being bored; handling old resentments, and so forth.

The goal(s) selected must be specific, simple, small, and, most important, achievable. Goal activities, of course, must be non-drug-related and should give the client feelings of pleasure and accomplishment. Examples of goal-oriented activities include walking in the park for thirty minutes twice a week; eating more nutritiously; taking food supplements; swimming; joining the YMCA or YWCA; taking up a new hobby or exercise, such as weight lifting; visiting a zoo; taking a friend to a movie.

To help your clients act upon their incentives, ask them to select something from their checklist. As soon as they have accomplished a goal, or even made any positive movement in dealing with the challenge selected, they should be encouraged to reward themselves. Exercises of this type give clients an opportunity to change their lifestyles and to continue to move in a positive direction toward recovery.

Handling Feelings

Addicts and alcoholics often use drugs and alcohol to achieve certain feelings that, ironically, turn out to be uncomfortable. Initially, the drug accomplishes what the clients are seeking, but later the drug turns on them and what they experience is not what they originally intended. Clinicians are well aware that those clients who use drugs and alcohol to handle feelings generally experience great difficulty in the recovery process.

DECLARE Therapy emphasizes that the client should face his or her feelings (such as anger, anxiety, joy, happiness, or depression) rather than avoid or mask them. Facing feelings is essential if the client is ever going to develop an effective coping style for living a happy and productive life. With this philosophy in mind, the following suggestions are offered:

■ Help your client learn to relax. In response to the stress involved, the client needs to learn to calm down without the use of drugs or alcohol. You can help your client by encouraging him/her to take a deep breath, hold it for a brief period, and then slowly release it. Once relaxed, the client is better prepared for the next procedure.

■ Ask your client, "What are you feeling?" "Are you happy?" (Fearful? Bored? Sad? Angry? Lonely? Anxious?)

■ Encourage your client to get in touch with his/her feelings. Ask the client to stay with the feeling(s) being experienced if at all possible. It is important, at this point, for the client to avoid obsessive and intrusive thoughts of drug/alcohol use, to prevent any unwanted feelings and to mitigate any feelings that are uncomfortable.

As a clinician, you should point out to your client that he/she can survive the experience without any use of drugs or alcohol. You should also try to help your client realize that if he/she will "hang in there" and not resort to the use of chemicals, the intensity of the unpleasant experience will generally decrease within a relatively short period of time.

■ Assist the client in substituting something for the use of drugs or alcohol. Encourage involvement in non-drug-related activities in which the client doesn't usually engage and which would be pleasant and comforting.

■ Reward your client's success. Compliment him/her for successfully managing this challenge in the recovery process. This simple and sincere form of feedback can have incredibly positive effects on the client's coping skills and ability to maintain the recovery pattern.

■ Encourage your client to perform an activity that responds in kind or intensity to the feelings associated with using. For example, should your client feel angry, encourage him/her to exercise or do something physical like hitting a baseball, shadow boxing, running, swimming, and so forth.

If the client expresses feelings of fatigue, a short energizing break from the day's routine may be helpful. Should the client indicate a sense of boredom, suggest some new and exciting activity for consideration. The idea here is for the activity to distract the client for a sufficiently long period of time that he/she will forget about using drugs or alcohol. In the event your client cannot identify specific feelings, any activity that he/she finds appealing may serve the purpose. If this activity does not prove to be effective in a short period of time, suggest an alternate one.

Inpatient Counseling

Despite the client's best efforts, there are times when clients will continue to have difficulty with expressing feelings, a situation that can have a negative impact on the recovery process. When this happens, the clinician should ask point-blank, "What is it that you wish to do?" Don't be surprised if your client says the only option is to begin using again. If this happens, you should suggest inpatient counseling services and make the appropriate referral.

Managing Stress

Unfortunately, our society presents many potentially stressful situations. There are individual differences, of course, in how each of us responds to stress, and what may be stressful for one person may not be stressful for another. Stress, then, may be defined as the individual response to the emotional and/or physical strain that is felt when a person faces challenges or demands.

Generally speaking, individuals experience conflict when they are confronted with two incompatible demands, opportunities, needs, or goals. Unfortunately, it is impossible to resolve such conflicts completely, and any effort toward resolution—be it to change or abandon a course of action—is bound to result in frustration and cause stress.

DECLARE Therapy offers several suggestions for helping the client reduce the stress related to recovery efforts. Stress reduction techniques encourage clients to identify the sources of stress in their daily lives and to take note of specific ways they experience it (Nash, 1976). Among the following suggested techniques, the reader will recognize procedures previously outlined in Chapter 2.

Journal Keeping

DECLARE Therapy encourages the client to keep a record of feelings, especially of negative ones, which can actually exacerbate the deleterious effects of stress on the body. The following instructions and questions (adapted from Nash, 1976) can be used in developing a journal or daily log:

- Take note of when you need the drug and/or alcohol.
- Where are you feeling the discomfort? Explain what it feels like.
- Take note of your surroundings. Who are you with? Where are you? What is going on while you are experiencing the discomfort?
- What is your first response to this discomfort? What do you want to do? Do you want to take a drug or escape your surroundings?
- What do you finally do?

Imagery and Self-Hypnosis

Imagery and self-hypnosis are useful techniques that can be taught to the abuser in a skill-based program designed to alter perceptions and images. The therapeutic use of self-hypnosis with drug clients depends on the acquisition and reinforcement of several important skills:

- Focusing attention
- Generating positive images
- Inducing a state of relaxed wakefulness (Kroger & Fezler, 1976)

Hypnotic techniques outlined by Kroger and Fezler (1976) for the treatment of drug abuse are based on repeatedly emphasizing, under hypnosis, the deleterious effects of drugs, the client's ability to control his or her own behavior, and, finally, the establishment of the client's emotional needs for the symptoms. The self-destructive drives uncovered during hypnosis should be channeled into healthy outlets, such as sports, hobbies, social activities, and other constructive endeavors.

Guided Imagery

Guided imagery is a technique of communication with internal unconscious processes that uses the power of the imagination to evoke specific psychological changes as an aid to therapy. Many clinicians today are experimenting with the creative use of mental imagery in behavior rehearsal, dream-drama, and other techniques.

The first step in imagery techniques is relaxation. Popular methods to achieve relaxation include:

- Meditation
- Progressive relaxation of the body muscle system, from head to toe
- Focusing on one's breathing while allowing all other thoughts to slip away or by recalling some pleasant setting. This image stimulates the body to relax and inhibits muscle activity as well as verbal thoughts, thereby permitting positive mental images to become dominant.

To assist the client in guided imagery, the therapist imagines a scene that he or she believes indicates the client's conflicts, fears, or desires for change. The therapist requires that the client project himself/herself into the scene and then describe it aloud.

The therapist then selects someone or something alive in the scene, other than the client, and directs the client to get in touch with this "inner adviser" (Sherman & Fredman, 1986). This "inner adviser" technique can be used whenever the client is experiencing trouble in handling a situation or making a choice or plan. The therapist has the "inner adviser" take the drug-abusing behavior unto itself and away from the client, seeking the client's agreement to do so. Finally, the client is directed to leave the state of relaxation and return to "normal."

Diversion Techniques

Diversion techniques are designed to divert the client's attention away from drugs/alcohol and toward something positive. Diversion may be accomplished in one of several different ways.

The client may be encouraged to get involved in physical activities such as jogging, swimming, bowling, or some structured exercise program. Another technique entails having the client carry three different objects in his/her pocket—for example, three coins (penny, nickel, and dime)—and to identify them, by touch, whenever thoughts of alcohol/drugs enter into consciousness.

Need for Support

The experience of recovery is much easier if clients have people in their lives who are supportive of their efforts. Such support can actually help increase the motivation level of clients, a particularly welcome effect when clients are experiencing difficulty in facing challenges.

Clients often express a need to be connected to someone because, in many cases, their bouts of drinking or drugging have driven away loved ones. On the other hand, lack of support can be particularly harmful to clients and may lead to the resumption of substance abuse.

It is critical, therefore, that clinicians assist clients in obtaining the information they need regarding support systems, and clinicians must not automatically assume their clients will find a support system on their own.

Selection of Support Persons

Like recovery itself, finding appropriate support is a process. First, the client needs to articulate what type of support is required, for what is supportive for one client is not necessarily supportive for another. The clinician can be of immense assistance in helping the client answer some difficult questions, such as:

- "What is best for me at this time in my recovery?"
- "What do I need to do to strengthen my resolve in order to remain sober?"
- "Who has supported me in the past?"

The sooner the client is able to articulate the answers to these questions, the sooner the selection of a viable support system can be identified and mobilized to help.

First, clients should be cautioned in their selection of those who will lend support. The basic rationale is that not everyone can be supportive of another, even among the members of one's own family. Certain questions, therefore, should be asked before a selection is made:

- Does this person understand the concept of the disease of chemical dependency?
- Does this person understand the commitment involved?
- Has this person been supportive in the past?
- Does he/she have the time needed for this kind of commitment?
- Is the person committed to helping the addict through recovery?
- Can this potential support person handle disappointment?

If the person in question cannot answer these questions in the affirmative, serious consideration should be given to selecting someone else.

As with other stages in DECLARE Therapy, in the selection of a support person the clinician should work with the client in determining specific needs. In other words, what does the client wish the support person to do? Clarifying needs in a realistic manner is the only way the client can hope to gain adequate assistance and support.

Effectiveness of Support

Throughout the recovery phase of therapy, clinicians must remind their clients to directly state that they are in recovery and need support. This is essential! Clients who refuse to make this admission, out of sense of embarrassment or pride, usually end up as failures. Until they are honest and open with others about their recovery efforts, they cannot expect others to be of any practical assistance.

Whenever clients receive the support they need, they should be encouraged to let their support persons know how much they are appreciated and how motivating it is to have them in their corner. They should also determine if their support persons are comfortable with the arrangement and if they need to make any substantial revisions in the relationship. Should any actual or potential problems be discovered at this time (especially situations that cannot be immediately resolved), consideration should be given to severing the relationship.

Support Meetings

During the recovery process, clinicians should encourage their clients to attend open and closed community meetings of groups such as Alcoholic Anonymous (AA), Narcotics Anonymous (NA) and Cocaine Anonymous (CA). Attendance at meetings of this type is important because it may provide indispensable support and encouragement, especially when the client is negotiating rough spots on the road to recovery or when other forms of support are not available. In fact, AA has proven to be an effective means of support for chemically dependent persons for more than half a century.

Members of groups such as AA, NA, and CA not only find a solid, supportive network, but are also offered a twelve-step program to guide them throughout their recovery. Through programs like this, many persons have entered into the recovery process without formal treatment. Affiliating with others who are having the same or similar experiences can motivate individuals recovering from chemical dependence to stay on the right path. Unequivocally, DECLARE Therapy regards Alcoholics Anonymous and other support groups with the highest esteem.

Managing Others Who Are Unsupportive

Persons in the recovery process sometimes find that others are not supportive in their efforts to remain sober. The reasons for this development vary from person to person and situation to situation. Among addicts and alcoholics, this situation often results in some form of desired change to "the way things used to be." Persons in recovery are often confronted with such "change messages" as:

- Why can't it be like it used to be?
- We had so much fun when we got high together.
- Let's get a bottle.
- Let's get this 8-ball.
- You ain't cool anymore.

At other times, lack of support may take the form of silence, as former drug-abusing friends of clients avoid them because they feel they can no longer be trusted. Regardless of what form this nonsupport takes, it can be upsetting to clients. In managing situations like this, they must try to remember the following:

■ Be aware that not everyone shares their views concerning recovery. To use an old football phrase, "The best offense is a good defense."

■ They should tell unsupportive individuals how they feel about their remarks. They should not, however, give in to their messages. Instead, they should attempt to indicate to the unsupportive persons how they can be of assistance during the recovery process.

Should these individuals continue to be unsupportive, clients might try following these suggestions:

■ Ignore the comments.
■ Be firm and say no!
■ Tell the unsupportive person, "I like the way I am today. You should try it."
■ Remind yourself and others, "That's not me anymore."
■ Tell anyone attempting to thwart your efforts, "Keep that stuff away from me."
■ Observe the four-second rule, GET OUT OF THERE!

It is also helpful to remind clients that if they remain firm in their resolve to stay clean and sober, such comments from unsupportive persons will subside and eventually disappear. However, should such attempts to hinder the recovery process continue, clients should simply stay away from these unsupportive individuals.

Craving

Craving may be defined as "a subjective experience of desiring, needing or longing for the euphoric and tension-relieving properties" of various mood-altering chemicals (Nace, 1987). The addict's craving for a drug is associated with dependence on it for relief of physical or psychological symptoms. Gradually, the repeated experience of using the drug to remove feelings of discomfort associated with withdrawal causes modifications in the addict's attitudes toward the drug and to the behaviors that constitute addiction. In effect, the addict becomes addicted to the *feeling* the drug produces and not to the drug per se. Therefore, the rapid heart beat, tremors, perspiration and/or anxiety that characterize withdrawal may trigger cravings when reexperienced in any given situation.

Wise (1984) has suggested that craving may be understood in the context of both positive and negative reinforcement. Positive reinforcement is produced by any stimulus that brings euphoria or pleasure to an individual in a normal state. Negative reinforcement, on the other hand, is caused by a stimulus that terminates distress or dysphoria and moves the person toward a normal state. Since a craving may result directly from a previous experience with a particular drug, a craving for a drug will vary in intensity depending on the addict's past memories, along with the presence of secondary reinforcing stimuli in the environment. As a result, a client may experience a craving when in the presence of people, places, or things associated with previous use.

Among drug addicts and alcoholics, cravings are extremely difficult to handle; and most chemically dependent persons develop intense fears regarding them. Many, in fact, believe that whenever a craving occurs, it is a signal that prognosis for recovery is hopeless. In situations like this, of course, clinicians must help the addict to understand that craving is not necessarily a sign of a poor prognosis. Clients should be encouraged to accept the notion that craving is a normal part of recovery, typical of persons who are coping with the struggle of abstinence.

Craving Intervention Plan

DECLARE Therapy offers a craving intervention plan designed to stop craving once it starts. As with other components of the model, this plan follows the acronym:

Dismantle euphoric recall

Euphoric recall refers to an addict's positive memories of experiences with drugs/alcohol. When haunted by such memories, the client must be warned that they only signal the impulse to use again. In other words, denial is alive and well and ready for action.

Escape the triggers

Clients should be reminded to become aware of various feelings and frustrations—mood changes, jealousy, boredom, loneliness, fatigue, hunger, fear, anger, tension, conflict, sexual difficulties, school and/or work problems, sleep disorders, health problems, legal problems, guilt, feelings of remorse, and so forth. Only when addicts are aware of such feelings and problems can they face their challenge. Being "tuned into" internal and external environments can give addicts a sense of power and control over their lives.

Change lifestyle and environment

All addicts must decide to make significant changes in their world, changes that signal a commitment to living a better life. Because of their addiction, they must make extra efforts to avoid persons, places, things, and situations that are associated with prior use.

Lose the fear of sobriety

Most addicts and alcoholics fear sobriety. They fear sobriety because they believe, incorrectly, that they can never stop using. To addicts or alcoholics, the notion of living without the drug(s) of choice is generally inconceivable. To them, this is a scary thought, one that creates high levels of anxiety. It is not unusual for addicts and alcoholics to dwell on their fears, wondering:

- What will I do with my time?
- What if I need something to help me over the rough spots?
- How will I have fun and enjoy myself if I'm not using? Life will be so boring.

The DECLARE therapist recognizes this fear in their clients and should assist them in resolving it.

Accept craving as normal
Drug addicts and alcoholics fear craving, because they believe that once the craving begins, they will not be able to refrain from use again. These persons must learn to realize that craving is a natural part of the struggle to achieve on-going sobriety. Clinicians must educate their clients to recognize and accept cravings as a natural occurrence in the recovery journey of every person with a substance-related disorder.

Relax and meditate
There are several ways to deal with the stresses that led to drug or alcohol abuse in the first place and that continue to plague those with substance-abuse-related disorders. These methods have all the benefits and none of the side effects of drinking and using drugs: diaphragmatic breathing exercising, visual imagery, and meditation.

Exercise
Addicts and alcoholics who become involved in daily, routine exercise programs expedite their recovery. Becoming physically active is a means of replenishing the valuable neurotransmitter substances in the brain that are depleted by drug abuse.

Exercise also has the added benefit of reducing the tension that accompanies stress. Becoming involved in physical activities such as mowing the lawn, swimming, riding a bike, walking, jogging, weight lifting, playing basketball, cleaning house, and so forth, can be very beneficial.

Relapses and Slips

DECLARE Therapy recognizes that sometimes the recovering alcoholic or addict may relapse. In fact, relapse is often part of the recovery process but does not mean that all is lost and that the client is doomed to return to a life of drug abuse. This type of unrealistic belief will only lead to feelings of hopelessness and powerlessness.

Relapse is defined as a period during which the client becomes either overconfident or underconfident and ends up losing control, often repeating old destructive behaviors. Relapse usually begins weeks or months prior to the actual resumption of use. In fact, resumption is simply the predictable final stage of a relapse episode (Marlatt & Gordon, 1985; Carroll, 1992; Baer et al., 1982). A slip, on the other hand, is considered a period during which the individual uses, but is not out of control.

It is important that the client understand what relapse is and what it is not. Relapses do not occur suddenly or without warning. They generally involve a gradual movement away from sobriety. An episode of relapse can be compared to an automobile tire slowing losing its air. The loss of air can be so slow that it is almost imperceptible.

The symptoms of relapse may begin with the client being tempted to believe that he or she has regained the control needed to use again (denial). This, of course, is very dangerous thinking, especially in the early stages of recovery. Whenever overconfidence like this sets in, it's time to recall the reasons why the client is in recovery in the first place.

DECLARE Therapy allows clients to exercise some control over their lives, particularly where relapse episodes are concerned. This is accomplished by providing the client with some early warning detection system to recognize relapses before they occur.

It should be emphasized to clients that a relapse is not just using drugs and alcohol. A relapse involves a set of symptoms that create an atmosphere conducive for the return of out-of-control use. As with other components of the DECLARE model, this warning system can be spelled out using the acronym.

Denial reactivated

Many clients, especially after a period of abstinence, falsely believe they can begin using again. "I know what I did wrong before . . . I know how to drink/drug now," they tell themselves. These clients need to know what's going on in their mind and avoid the thoughts that they can return to drinking/drugging without serious consequences.

Early warning signs

Before they lose control, clients should be taught to interrupt early warning signs of relapse by asking questions such as, "What does it mean when I'm irritable or feeling depressed?" "What does it mean when I'm angry?" Unfortunately, many addicts and alcoholics are unable to interpret these warning signs because they are already out of control.

Control

Clients must be encouraged to regain self-control over their thoughts, judgment, emotions, memory, and behavior. In most cases, they must also be taught how to do this. The first step is calming down. Clients should try the following exercise:

Take a deep breath and hold, then exhale slowly. Repeat this as many times as necessary.

Thinking about using drugs and alcohol is very dangerous because it usually places the individual in situations in which use is likely to occur. Often clients permit themselves to be placed in situations in which drugs and alcohol are available. Somehow, addicts believe that this proves they can handle the substance(s) without using them.

Clients experiencing relapse should be reminded that no one is perfect and that they should give themselves praise for having tried and forgiveness for having failed. They should also be taught that they can learn from the experience and move on, setting new standards and expectations for the future. In such situations, clients can often regain control by challenging and replacing the negative thought(s) and behavior(s).

Listing warning signs

Clients should be advised to make a list of any warning signs that could signal relapse—things such as tension, mood changes, conflicts with family and friends, sexual difficulties, problems on the job or at school, financial problems, health concerns, legal difficulties, feelings of guilt and remorse, and cravings.

Acting on what others say

Clients should be reminded that they cannot recover in isolation, as they often cannot realistically see what is happening. They need others for support.

Relapse education

It is important that clients fully understand the relapse process. To this end, they should educate themselves, talk with other drug addicts and alcoholics, and learn as much as they can about the experiences they have regarding relapse. By increasing awareness, clients have a better-than-even chance of preventing relapse.

Entries

It is important that clients review their daily diary or journal.

Managing Change

When clients decide to change and make a commitment to a different lifestyle consistent with recovery, they open the door to a new world full of challenges and choices. How clients manage these challenges and choices will ultimately determine whether they will return to drinking and drugging or will recover. The choice ultimately rests with each client.

As clinicians, we can only guide these persons, providing encouragement, support, and hope. When we work as a team, counselor and client, with mutual respect and basic human kindness, we can all be successful. Indeed the final letter we must recall in the client-therapist struggle for sobriety is the Churchillian **V** and all it stands for. This chapter brings us, in effect, full circle. As we saw in Chapter 1 and its discussion of the Churchill Syndrome, and as emphasized throughout the book, the journey to recovery is eminently and poignantly human.

Recapping . . .

- Recovery is not a destination. It is a journey—one that takes time.
- This journey consists of meeting challenges, making choices and, eventually, experiencing the joy of a new life.
- Recovery involves a seven-step process. In facing recovery challenges, clients must:

    D. Decide if they really want recovery
    E. Establish a challenge checklist
    C. Choose what works for them
    L. Lose the fear of recovery
    A. Act upon the plan they have established
    R. Record results
    E. Evaluate results

- Because recovering alcoholics and addicts often have unrealistic expectations about recovery, clients should be assisted with putting their situation in perspective, developing incentives for remaining sober, facing and vocalizing their feelings, and developing stress management and relaxation techniques.
- DECLARE therapy encourages clients to keep a journal, to develop diversion techniques to prevent returning to drugs/alcohol, and to seek support from family, friends, and organized support groups.
- DECLARE Therapy offers a craving intervention plan to help clients stop craving once it starts. As in other components of the model, the acronym references the steps involved:

    D. Dismantle euphoric recall
    E. Escape the triggers
    C. Change lifestyle and environment
    L. Lose the fear of sobriety
    A. Accept craving as normal
    R. Relax and meditate
    E. Exercise

- How clients manage the challenges and choices involved in the journey of recovery will ultimately determine whether they will return to drinking/drugging or will recover. The choice, of course, ultimately rests with each client.
- As clinicians, we can only guide these persons, providing encouragement, support, and hope, confident in our realization that implicit in the DECLARE acronym is the letter **V** and the hard-won struggle it symbolizes.

Epilogue

Life is a both a precious gift and a journey—a journey toward the fullness and richness of living, which is ours by our very birthright.

For the recovering addict, the journey includes special challenges and choices. As this text has indicated (and as I have been gratified to witness with numerous clients over the years), the journey can be exhilarating and the battle over drug, alcohol, and other addictions (gambling, sex, etc.) can be won.

Using the DECLARE approach and encouraging our clients to tap into their spirituality and inner strength, we clinicians can encourage and guide them toward healthy, happy, and productive lives.

This is both the challenge and the joy of our rewarding profession. May you be energized by the hills and the valleys, the setbacks, and the victories as you continue along your journeys—both personal and professional.

Bibliography

Alcoholics Anonymous (1976). *Alcoholics Anonymous World Services.* New York: Author.

Allen, M., & Frances, R. (1986). Varieties of psychopathology found in patients with addictive disorders: A review. In R. Myer (Ed.), *Psychopathology and addictive disorders* (pp. 17–38). New York: Guilford.

Alterman, A. (1985). Relationship between substance abuse and psychopathology: Overview. In A. Alterman (Ed.), *Substance abuse and psychopathology* (pp. 1–14). New York: Plenum Press.

Alterman, A. I., McDermott, P. A., Cacciola, J. J., Rutherford, M. J., Boardman, C. R., McKay, J. R., & Cook, T. G. (1998). A typology of antisociality in methedone patients. *Journal of Abnormal Psychology, 107*(2), 412–422.

American Psychiatric Association (2000). Diagnostic and Statistical Manual of Mental Disorders (4th ed., Text Revision). Washington, D.C.: Author.

Baer, J. S., Marlatt, G. A., Kivlahan, D. R., Fromme, K., Larimer, M. E., & Williams, E. (1982). An experimental test of three methods of alcohol risk reduction with young adults. *Journal of Consulting and Clinical Psychology, 60,* 974–979.

Beck, A. T., Rush, A. J., Shaw, B. F., & Emery, G. (1979). *Cognitive Therapy of Depression.* New York: Guilford.

Beck, A. T. (1982). *Cognitive theory of depression: New perspectives.* In P. Clayton & Barrett (eds.), Treatment of depression: Old controversies and new approaches. New York: Raven.

Bellissimo, A. A., & Tunks, E. (1984). *Chronic pain: The psychotherapeutic spectrum.* New York: Praeger.

Bender, L. (1978). A visual motor gestalt test and its clinical use. *American Orthopsychiatric Association Research Monograph,* No. 3.

Bernstein, D. A., & Borkover, T. D. (1975). *Progressive relaxation training: A manual for the helping professions.* Champaign, IL: Research Press.

Bootzin, R. R., Acocella, J. R., & Alloy, L. B. (1993). *Abnormal Psychology: Current Perspective* (6th Ed.). New York: McGraw-Hill.

Brill, L. (1981). *The clinical treatment of substance abusers.* Free Press: Macmillan.

Brown, H. P., Jr., & Peterson, J. H., Jr. (1990). Rationale and procedural suggestions for defining and actualizing spiritual values in the treatment of dependency. *Alcoholism Treatment Quarterly, 7*(3), 17–46.

Califano, J. A. (1979). "Presentation by Joseph A. Califano before the National Council on Alcoholism." *Alcoholism: Clinical and Experimental Research* 3, 368–373.

Carroll, K. M. (1992). Psychotherapy for cocaine use: Approaches, evidence and conceptual models. In T. R. Kosten & H. D. Kleber (Ed.). *Clinician's guide to cocaine addiction: Theory, research, and treatment* (pp. 220–313). New York: Guilford Press.

Chasnoff, I. J. (1988). Drug use in pregnancy: Parameters of risk. *Pediatric Clinics of North America, 35*(6), 1403–12.

Chasnoff, I. J. (2002). *Drug use in pregnancy: Mother and child.* Boston: Kluwer.

Cloninger, C. (1988). *Biological vulnerability to drug abuse.* (Research Monograph No. 89, pp. 52–72). Rockville, MD: National Institute on Drug Abuse.

Craig, R. J. (1987). *Clinical management of substance abuse programs.* Springfield, IL: Thomas.

Eimer, B. N. (1988). The chronic pain patient: Multimodal assessment & psychotherapy. *International Journal of Medical Psychotherapy.* 1, 23–40

Ellison, C. G. (1991). Religious involvement and subjective well-being. *Journal of Health and Social Behavior, 32,* 80–99.

Elkind, D., & Weiner, I. (1978). *Development of the child.* New York: Wiley.

French, M. T., Mauskapf, J. A., Teague, J. L., & Roland, E. J. (1996). Estimating the dollar value of health outcomes from drug-abuse interventions. *Medical Care, 34,* 890–910.

Gilbert, J. G., & Lombardi, D. N. (1967). Personality characteristics of young male narcotic addicts. *Journal of Counseling Psychology, 31,* 536–538.

Glynn, T., Pearson, H. W., & Sayers, M. (1983). Women and drugs. *Research Issues,* 31. Rockville, MD: National Institute of Drug Abuse.

Gold, M. S. (1987). Crack abuse: Its implications and outcomes, *Resident and Staff Physician, 33.*

Goode, E. (1973). *The drug phenomenon: Social aspects of drug taking.* Indianapolis: Bobbs-Merrill.

Goodwin, D. W., & Gabrielli, W. F. (1997). Alcohol: Clinical aspects. In J. H. Lowinson, P. Ruiz, R. B. Millman, & J. G. Langrod (Eds.). *Substance abuse: A Comprehensive textbook* (pp. 142–148). Baltimore: Williams & Wilkins.

Graham, J. R. (1990). *MMPI-2: Assessing personality and psychopathology.* Oxford University Press.

Green, R. L. (1980). The MMPI: An Interpretive Manual. New York: Grime and Stratton.

Hathaway, S. R., & McKinley, J. (1943). *Manual for the Minnesota Multiphasic Personality Inventory.* New York: Psychological Corporation.

Haverkos, H., & Millstein, R. A. (1992). Development of theoretically based psychosocial therapies for drug dependence. Program announcement PA 92–110, Catalogue of federal domestic assistance No. 93.279. Department of Health and Human Services, Public Health Services. National Institute on Drug Abuse.

Inciardi, J. (1986). *The war on drugs: Heroin, cocaine, crime, and public policy.* Mountain View, CA: Mayfield.

Jarusiewicz, B. (2000). Spirituality and addiction: relationship to recovery. *Alcoholism Treatment Quarterly, 18*(4), 99–110.

Johnson, E. (1993). The role of spirituality in recovery from chemical dependency. *Journal of Addictions and Offender Counseling, 13*(2), 58–62.

Keith, G., MacGregor, S., Rosner, M., Chasnoff, I. J., & Sciarra, J. J. (1989). Substance abuse in pregnant women: Recent experience at the Perinatal Center for Chemical Dependency of Northwestern Memorial Hospital. *Obstetrics and Gynecology 73*(5) pp. 715–720.

Kroger, W. S., & Fezler, W. D. (1976). *Hypnosis and behavior modification: Imagery conditioning.* Philadelphia: Lippincott.

Kurtz, E. (1979). *Not God: A history of Alcoholics Anonymous.* Center City, MN: Hazelden. 48–49.

Koster, T. R., & Rounsaville, B. J. (1986). Psychopathology in opioid addicts. *Psychiatric Clinics of North America, 9,* 515–532.

Lazarus, A. A. (1981). *The practice of multimodal therapy: Systematic, comprehensive, and effective psychotherapy.* New York: McGraw-Hill.

Lazarus, A. A. (1985a). A brief overview of multimodal therapy. *Casebook of Multimodal Therapy.* New York: Guilford.

Lazarus, A. A. (1985b). The specificity factor in psychotherapy. *Casebook of Multimodal Therapy.* New York: Guilford.

Leshner, A. I. (1999). Science-based views of drug addiction and its treatment. *Journal of the American Medical Association, 282*(14), 1314–1316.

Lezak, M. D. (1983). *Neuropsychological Assessment.* New York: Oxford University Press.

Lubin, B., Brady, K., Woodward, L., & Thomas, E. A. (1986). Graduate professional psychology training in alcoholism and substance abuse. *Professional Psychology Research and Practice, 17*(2), 151–154.

Marlatt, G. A., & Gordon, J. R. (Ed.). (1985). *Relapse Prevention: Maintenance strategies in the treatment of addictive behaviors.* New York: Guilford.

Matsunaga, S. (1983). The federal role in research, treatment, and prevention of alcoholism. *American Psychologist, 38.*

Mayer, W. (1983). Alcohol abuse and alcoholism: The psychologist's role in prevention, research, and treatment. *American Psychologist, 38,* 1116–1121.

Meichenbaum, D. (1977). *Cognitive-behavior modification: An integrative approach.* New York: Plenum Press.

Metzger, L. (1988). *From denial to recovery: Counseling problem drinkers, alcoholics, and their families.* San Francisco: Jossey-Bass.

Meyer, R. E., & Mirin, S. M. (1979). *The heroin stimulus: Implications for a theory of addiction.* New York: Plenum.

Miller, N. (1991). Drug and alcohol addiction as a disease. *Alcohol Treatment Quarterly, 8,* 43–55.

Miller, W. R., & Hester, R. K. (1980). Treating the problem drinker: Modern approaches. In Miller, W. R. (Ed.) *The addictive behaviors: Treatment of alcoholism, drug abuse, smoking and obesity.* New York: Plenum Press.

Miller, W. R., & Hester, R. K. (1986). Inpatient alcoholism treatment: Who benefits? *American Psychologist, 41*(7), 794–805.

Nace, E. P. (1987). *The treatment of alcoholism.* New York: Brunner/Mazel.

Nahas, G. G., & Frick, H. C. (1981). *Drug abuse in the modern world: A perspective for the eighties.* New York: Pergamon.

Nash, J. D. (1976). Risk Factors Interventions: Stanford Heart Disease Prevention Program. *Stanford Disease Prevention Program, Stanford University.* (June), 2–12.

National Institute on Drug Abuse. Retrieved October 13, 2003, from the World Wide Web: http://www.nida.nih.gov/infofax/treatmeth.html.

Perls, F., Hefferline, R. F., & Goodman, P. (1951). *Gestalt Therapy.* New York: Julian Press.

Pickens, R. W., & Svikis, D. S., (eds.) (1988). *Biological Vulnerability to Drug Abuse.* NIDA Research Monograph 89. Rockville, MD: National Institute on Drug Abuse.

Pruzensky, Thomas. (1988). Collaboration of plastic surgeon and medical psychotherapist: Elective cosmetic surgery. *Medical Psychotherapy: An International Journal, 1,* 1–14.

Quayle, J. D. (1983). American productivity: the devastating effect of alcoholism and drug abuse. *American Psychologist, 38,*(4) 454–458.

Rorschach, H. (1942). *Psychodiagnostics: A diagnostic test based on perception* (P. Lemkau & B. Kronenberg, Trans.). Berne, Switzerland: Hans Huber.

Sherman, R., & Fredman, N. (1986). *Handbook of structured techniques in marriage and family therapy.* New York: Brunner Mazel.

Schuckit, M. A. (1989). *Drug and alcohol use: A clinical guide to diagnosis and treatment.* New York: Plenum.

Sperry, L. (2001). *Spirituality in clinical practice: Incorporating the spiritual dimension in psychotherapy and counseling.* Philadelphia: Brunner-Routledge.

Talbott, D. (1982). *An addictionologist defines chemical dependency.* Atlanta, GA: National Symposium on Psychiatry/Chemical Dependency.

Taylor, P., Jr. (1982). *Psychoactive drugs.* Minneapolis, Minn.: Burgess.

Taylor, P., Jr. & Lehrer, B. (1977). *New projective technique for assessing stress in college students.* ERIC Document, *Resources in Education.*

Taylor, P., Jr. (1988a). *Multifaceted Assessment of Chemical Dependency (MAC-D) Inventory.* Cincinnati, OH: Taylor Institute for Chemical Dependency.

Taylor, P., Jr. (1988b). *Substance abuse: pharmacologic and development perspective.* Springfield, IL: Thomas.

Taylor, P., Jr. (1988c). *Biphasic analysis reintegration sequence.* Cincinnati, OH: Taylor Institute for Chemical Dependency.

Taylor, P., Jr. (1988d). *Taylor historical questionnaire.* Cincinnati, OH: Taylor Institute for Chemical Dependency.

Taylor, P., Jr. (1990). DECLARE therapy: A new treatment approach for substance abuse and chemical dependency. *The Advocate: American Mental Health Counselor's Association Journal, 14(2).*

Taylor, P., Jr. (ed.) (1993). *Drug abuse.* Selected chapters from *Drugs in American Society,* (4th ed.) by Erich Goode; and *Drugs: A factual account,* (5th ed.) by Dorothy E. Dusek and Daniel A. Girdano. New York: McGraw-Hill.

Turk, D. C., Meichenbaum, D., & Genest, M. (1983). *Pain and behavior medicine: A cognitive-behavioral perspective.* New York: Guilford Press.

U.S. Department of Health and Human Services. (1991). *Health and behavior research.* National Institutes of Health: Reports to Congress.

Van de Bor, M., Walther, F. J., & Sims, M. E. (1990). Increased cerebral blood flow velocity in infants of mothers who abuse cocaine. *Pediatrics 85*(5): 733–736.

Wagner, E. E. (1983). *The hand test manual—Revised.* Los Angeles: Western Psychological Services.

Wallace, W. A. (1986). *Theories of counseling and psychotherapy: A basic-issues approach.* Boston: Allyn & Bacon.

Warfield, R. D., & Goldstein, M. B. (1996). Spirituality: The key to recovery from alcoholism. *Counseling and Values, 40*(3), 196–205.

Wechsler, D. (1981). *Manual for the Wechsler Adult Intelligence Scale—Revised.* San Antonio, TX: Psychological Corporation.

Weston, D. R., Ivins, B., Zuckerman, B., Jones, C., & Lopez, R. (1989). Drug exposed babies: Research and clinical issues. *Zero to Three: Bulletin of the National Center for Clinical Infant Programs, 9*(5).

Whitfield, C. L. (1984). Stress management and spirituality during recovery: A transpersonal approach Part I: Becoming. *Alcoholism Treatment Quarterly, 1*(1), 3–54.

Whitfield, C. L. (1985). Alcoholism, other drug problems, & spirituality: A transpersonal approach. Baltimore, MD: The Resource Group.

Wise, R. A. (1984). Neural mechanisms of the reinforcing action of cocaine. In: Grabowski, J., ed. *Cocaine: Pharmacology, Effects, and Treatment of Abuse.* National Institute on Drug Abuse Research Monograph 50. DHHS Pub. No. (ADM)87-1326. Washington, DC: Supt. of Docs. U.S. Govt. Print. Off. 15–33.

Worchel, S., & Shebilske, W. (1992). *Psychology: Principles and applications* (4th ed.). Englewood Cliffs, NJ: Prentice-Hall.

Zinnbauer, B. J., & Pargament, K. I. (2000). Working with the sacred: Four approaches to religious and spiritual issues in counseling. *Journal of Counseling & Development, 78,* 162–171.

Index